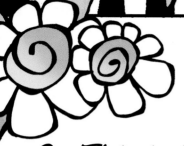

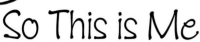

So This is Me

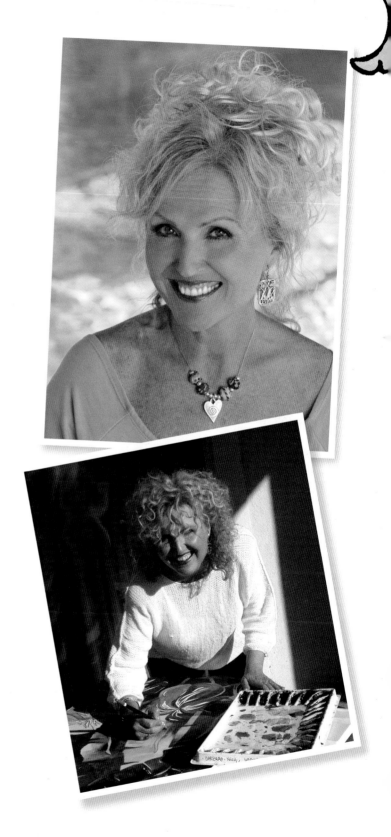

So this is me...I'm a tad wacky and just shy of crazy.

And I love to create. Whether I'm painting fine art in my studio, drawing my wacky characters on location at shows, sitting at my pottery wheel on my back porch, or writing at my computer, the creative process is liberating beyond words. I am forever exploring new ways to express the energy inside me. But I feel forever blessed to have these gifts and vow to never take them for granted.

I'm 50-something years old and live mere feet from the ocean in a funky little surf town called New Smyrna Beach, Florida. Yes, I know. New Smyrna Beach has been officially declared the "Shark Bite Capital of the World," but the sand sparkles like white crystals and the water is a thousand shades of aqua blue. Waking up every morning to this glorious sight makes my heart tingle. I share that space with my husband, Al, and a goofy Labrador retriever named Lucy. I eat chocolate truffles while I paint—and when they run out, I quit. I drink Perrier sparkling water so often I'm considering taking out stock in the company. I practice yoga, which for some strange reason I think will help compensate for my horrible diet, and I sit on the beach with my toes in the sand every chance I get.

I have five grown children and fourteen grandkids who love me as much as I adore them. I've taught them to dip their French fries in their chocolate shakes, make up any words they want to any tune they like, and to never, ever color inside the lines. (However, they all feel the need to assure their friends that they also have another set of grandparents who are "normal.")

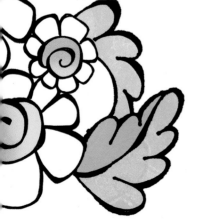

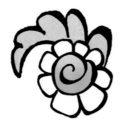

Here are some examples of my wacky characters and other work that I have painted with my favorite medium, watercolors.

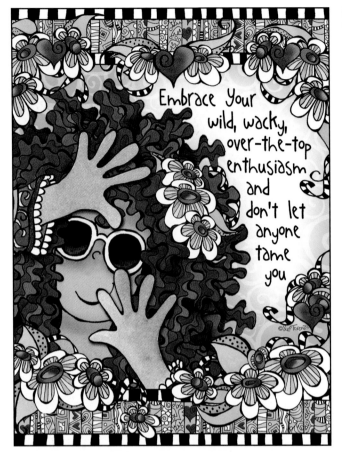

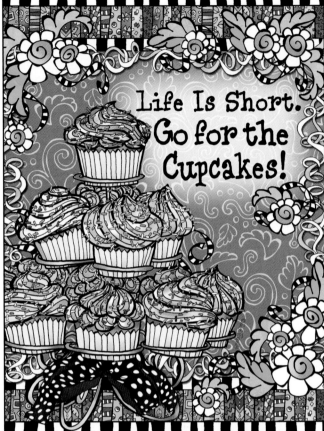

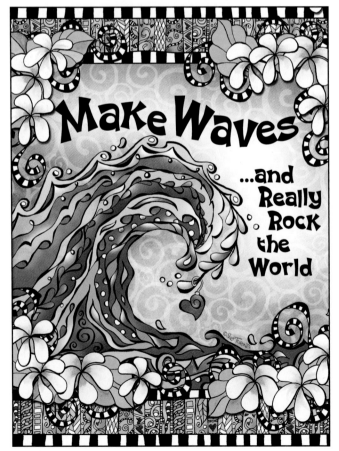

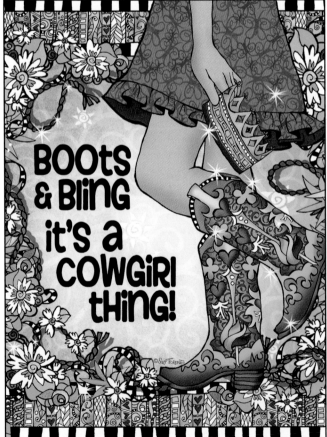

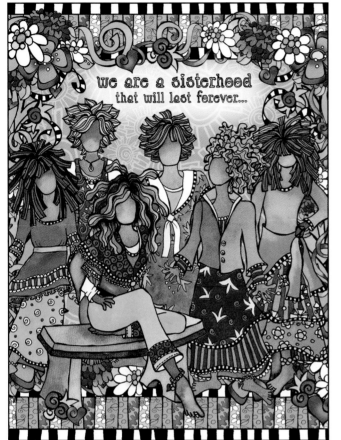

we are a sisterhood
that will last forever...

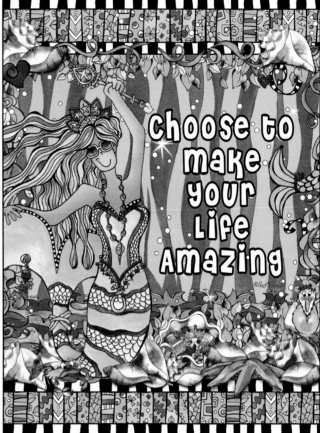

choose to
make
your
life
Amazing

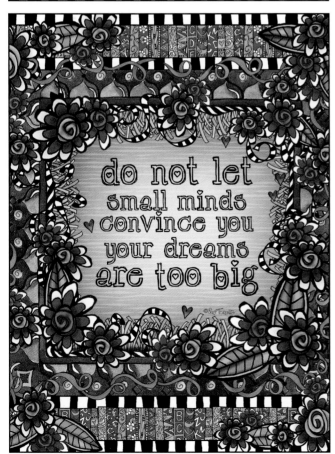

do not let
small minds
convince you
your dreams
are too big

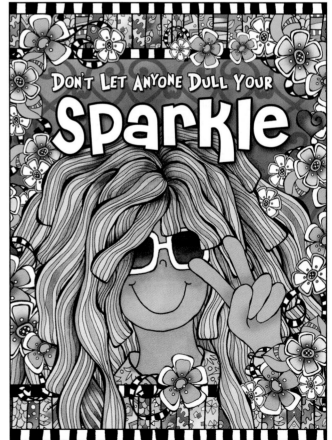

DON'T LET ANYONE DULL YOUR
Sparkle

Add the Color...
Feel the Tingle

There's nothing more satisfying than finishing a work of art. It adds excitement and joy to your life. Or to use my favorite tag line, you "Feel the Tingle."

The fact is, not everyone likes to draw, but everybody loves to color. Thus, anyone can experience the joy of participating in creating a piece of art with a coloring book. That's the genius of the medium. It's fun, interesting, and very fulfilling.

It doesn't matter how creative you are, you can learn about color and finish a masterpiece worth displaying. That's the purpose of this introduction—to teach you this skill.

If you already know this stuff, have a ball. If you don't, this information is way worth the effort. It will influence the way you color your entire world, from your home to your clothing to your food. Yes, even how you apply your makeup. And you will become a coloring book guru to boot.

So let's begin.

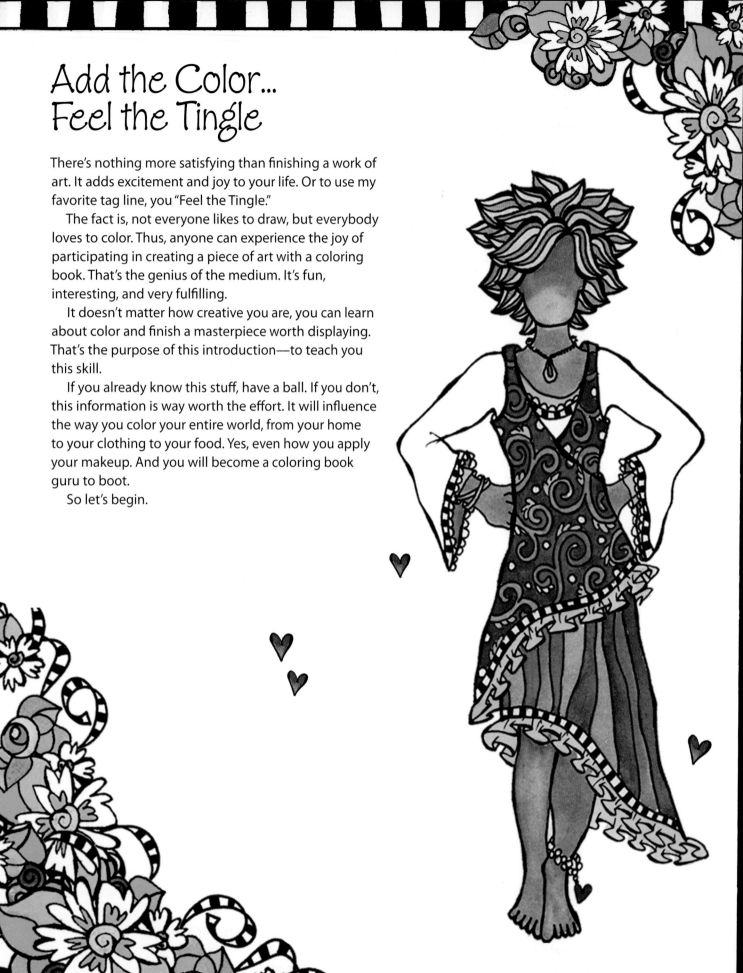

Color Selection Is Critical

You definitely want that "wow" factor when you're finished. So you need to know which colors do and do not complement each other. Do it right, and it will look like a Picasso.

The most essential tool in color selection is the color wheel, presented to the right. Each color in the wheel is either PRIMARY, SECONDARY, or TERTIARY.

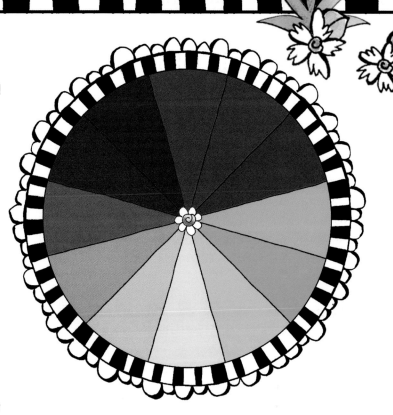

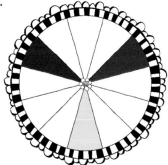

The primary colors are red, yellow, and blue. These are the root colors—they can't be created by mixing other colors. They are the pure foundation of the color wheel. All other colors are some combination of these three.

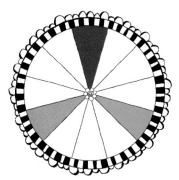

The secondary colors are orange, green, and purple. They are simply an equal mix of two primary colors (red + yellow = orange, yellow + blue = green, and blue + red = purple).

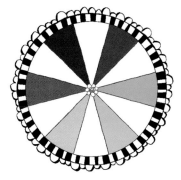

Tertiary colors are created by mixing a primary color with a secondary color. The resulting color is a matter of the percentage of the colors in the mix. There is no end to tertiary colors.

Colors are also categorized as warm or cool. Red, yellow, and orange are warm colors. Green, blue, and purple are cool colors. Selecting warm or cool colors really sets the mood of your piece. Warm colors are bold and exciting, while cool colors are more calm and peaceful.

Things really get interesting when you start playing with variations of a color. You can "tint" a color by adding white to the mix. Or you can "shade" a color by adding black.

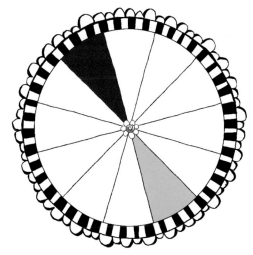

Colors opposite each other on the color wheel are called "complementary" and really pop off the page when they are used adjacent to each other. That's why you see yellow writing on purple backgrounds on billboards all over town. Or vice versa.

My Personal Twist

Since my earliest days as an artist, I have embraced the color yellow. Whether I am painting in my preferred medium of watercolors or dabbling in acrylics, pencils, markers, inks, or crayons, I almost always start with a layer of pale yellow—especially on a piece I want to be on the warm side of the color wheel. This assures that any work of art gets a wash of sunshine, whether the final colors are green, yellow, orange, or red. It really makes the colors pop. Greens get limey, oranges get a tangerine glow, reds get fiery, and yellows get even more electric.

And don't forget to leave open spaces with no color for white. It's easy to want to color every single nook and cranny with one of your fun colors, but leaving enough white is just as important to give your finished piece a lovely balance.

This is how I add a unique touch that is totally me. You should experiment with your own ways to make the art feel uniquely you! You might do this with your color choices or by adding patterns and flourishes to the art (check out the open spaces at the top and bottom of each piece, perfect for patterning). Have fun playing around!

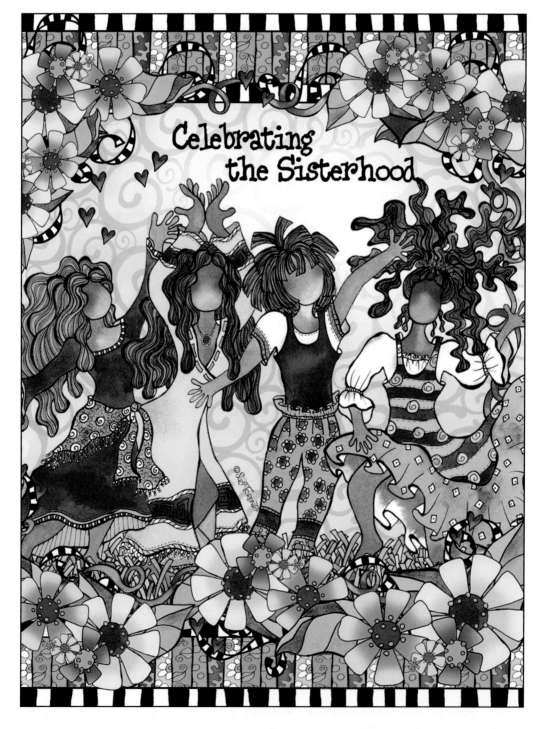

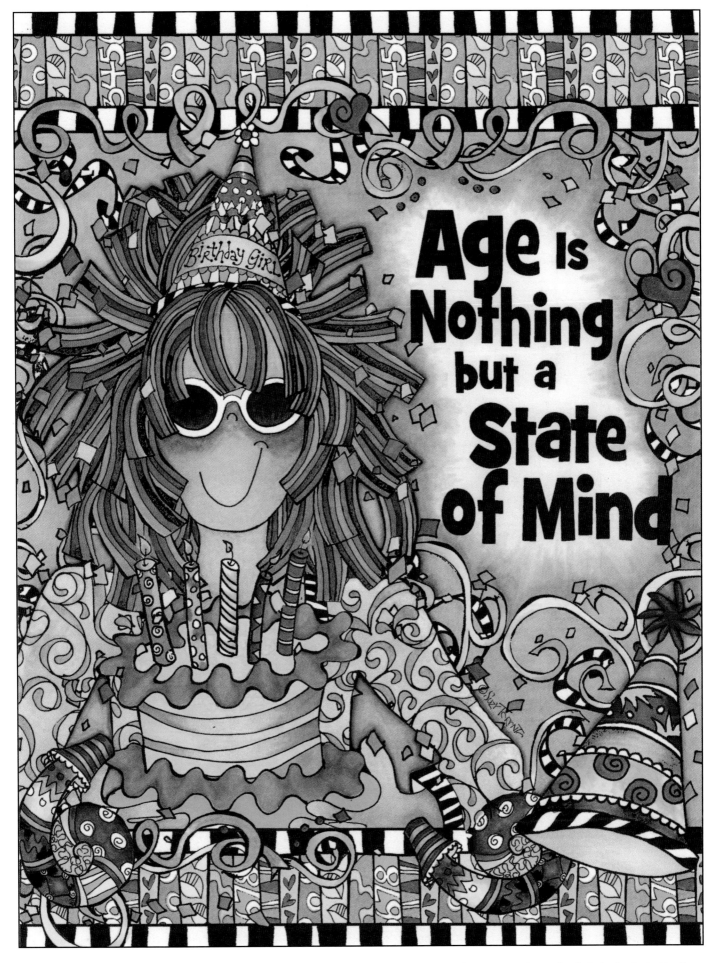

Age Is Nothing but a State of Mind

A State of Mind (Light & Laughter), Color by Cathy Pemberton

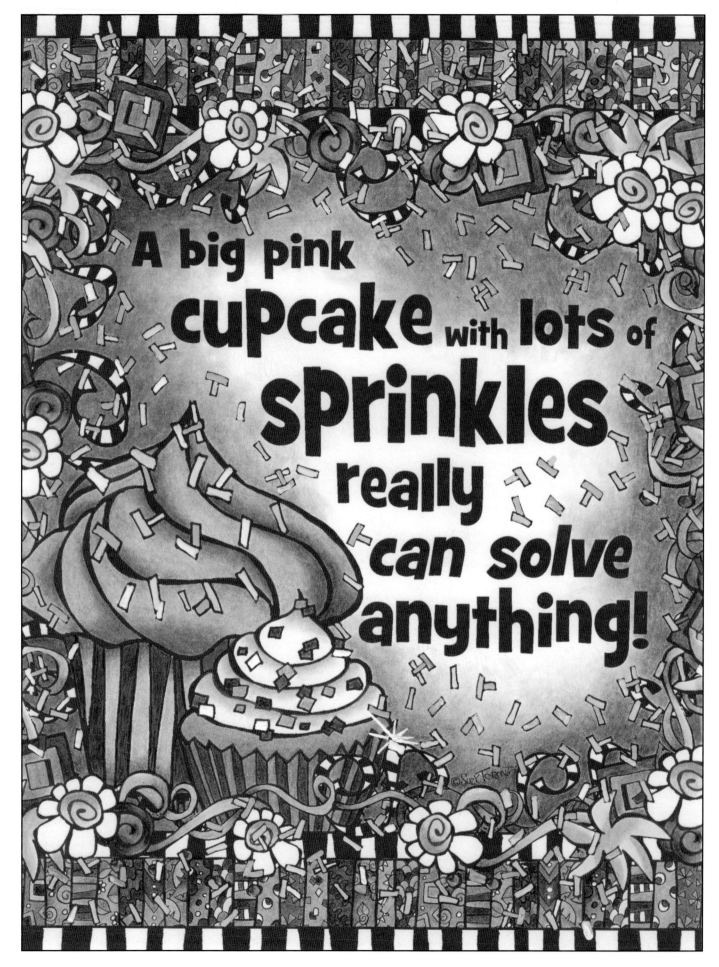

A big pink cupcake with lots of sprinkles really can solve anything!

Big Pink Cupcake, Color by Cathy Pemberton

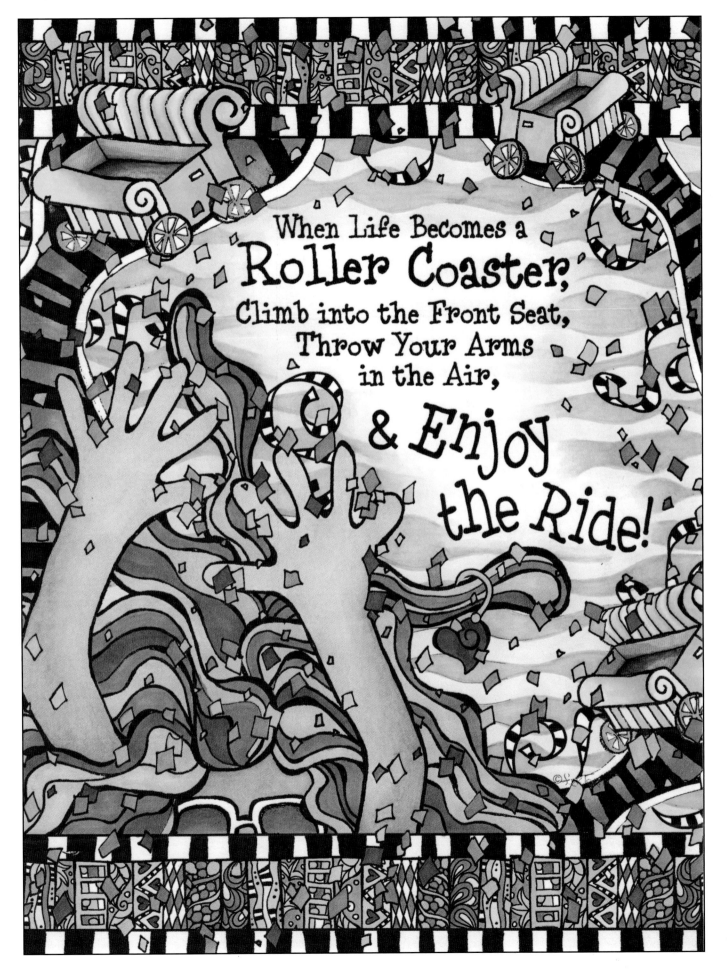

When Life Becomes a **Roller Coaster,** Climb into the Front Seat, Throw Your Arms in the Air, & Enjoy the Ride!

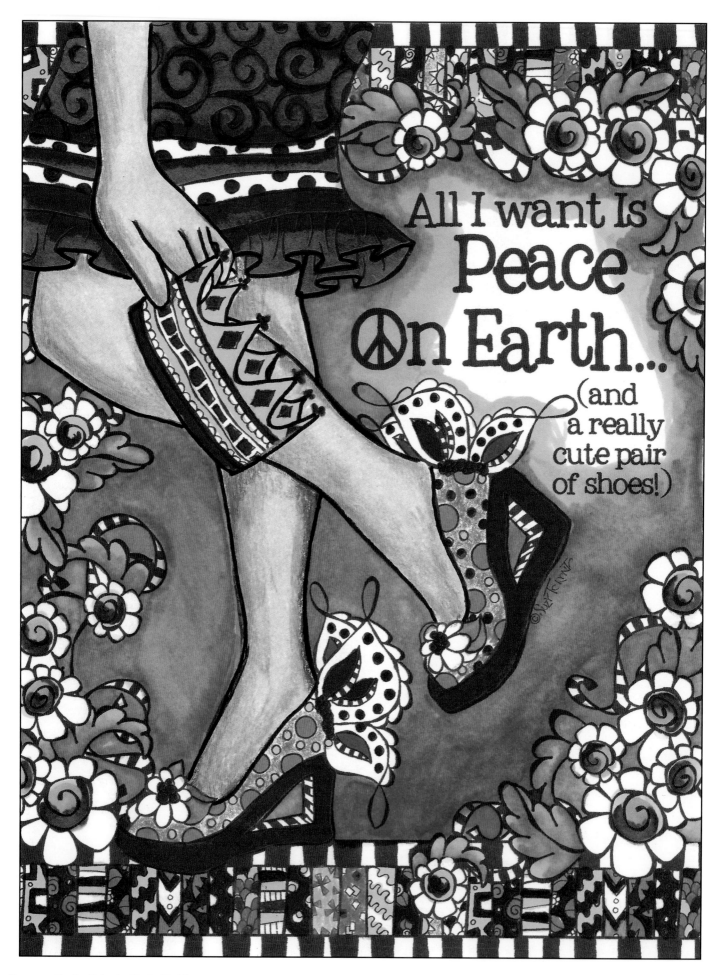

All I want Is **Peace ☮n Earth...** (and a really cute pair of shoes!)

Peace on Earth, Color by Emily Maddsen

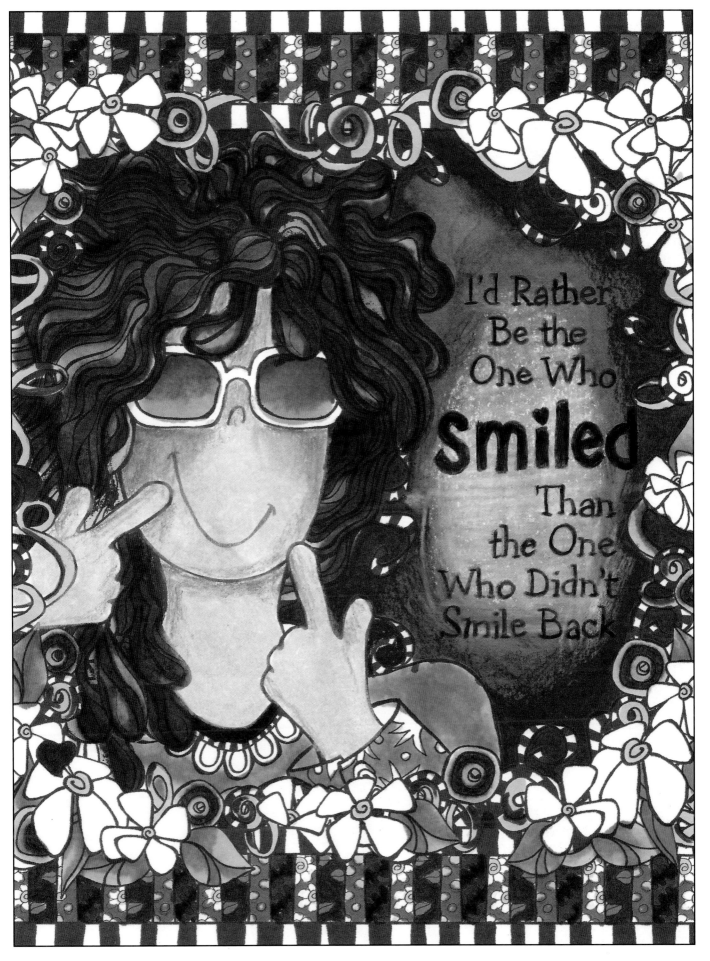

I'd Rather Be the One Who **Smiled** Than the One Who Didn't Smile Back

Be the One Who Smiled, Color by Emily Maddsen

©Suzy Toronto • suzytoronto.com • From *Light & Laughter Coloring Book* ©Design Originals, www.D-Originals.com

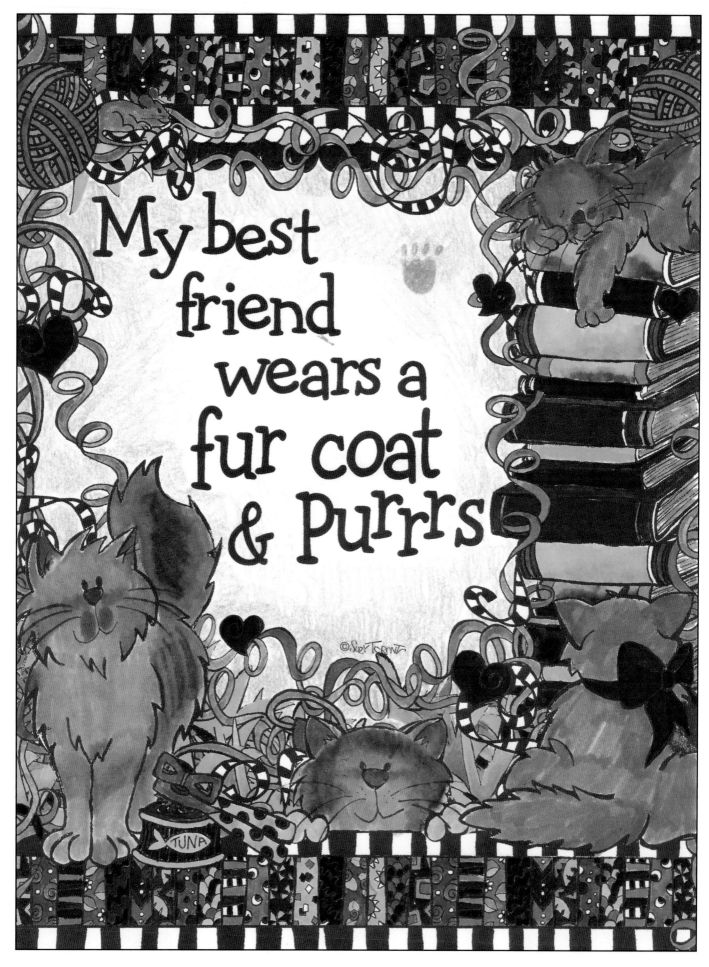

My best friend wears a fur coat & Purrs

©Suzy Toronto

My Best Friend Purrs, Color by Emily Maddsen

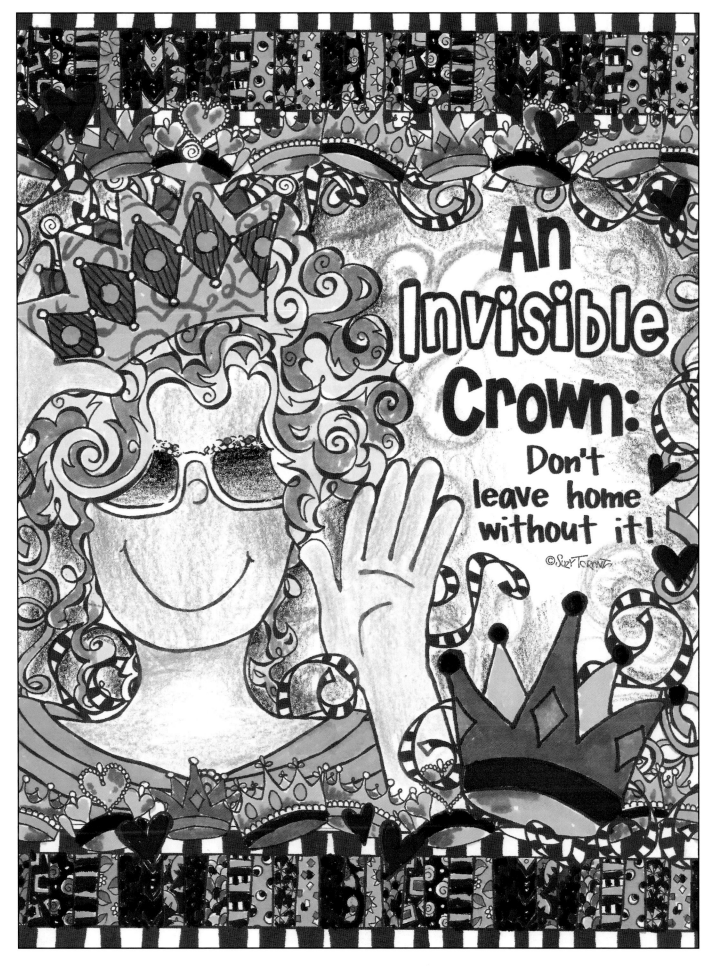

An Invisible Crown: Don't leave home without it!
©Suzy Toronto

Invisible Crown, Color by Emily Maddsen

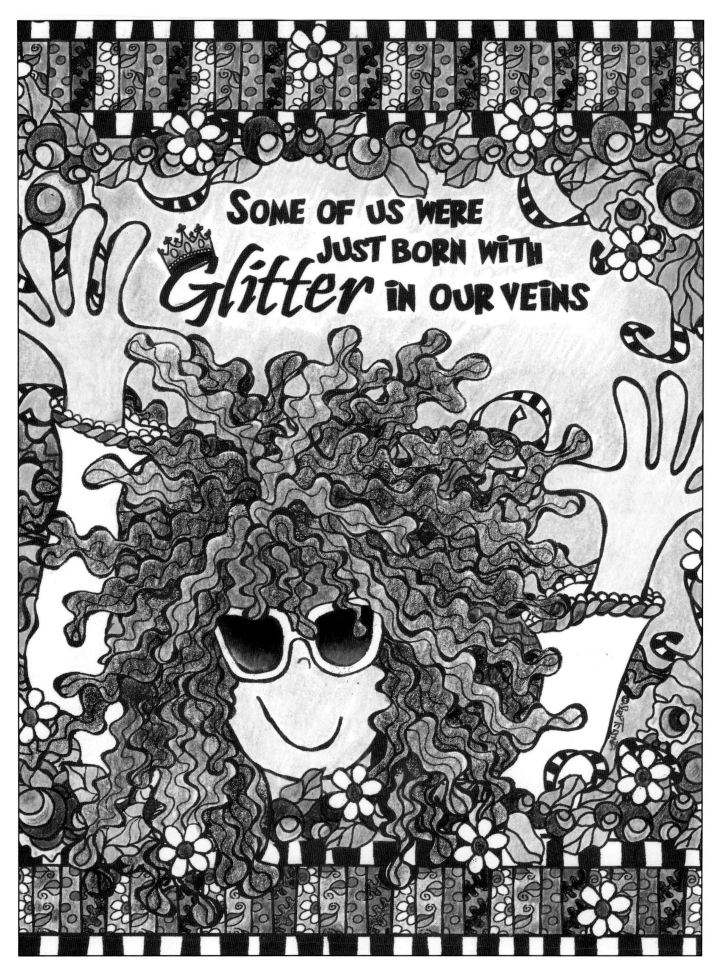

Born with Glitter, Color by Emily Maddsen

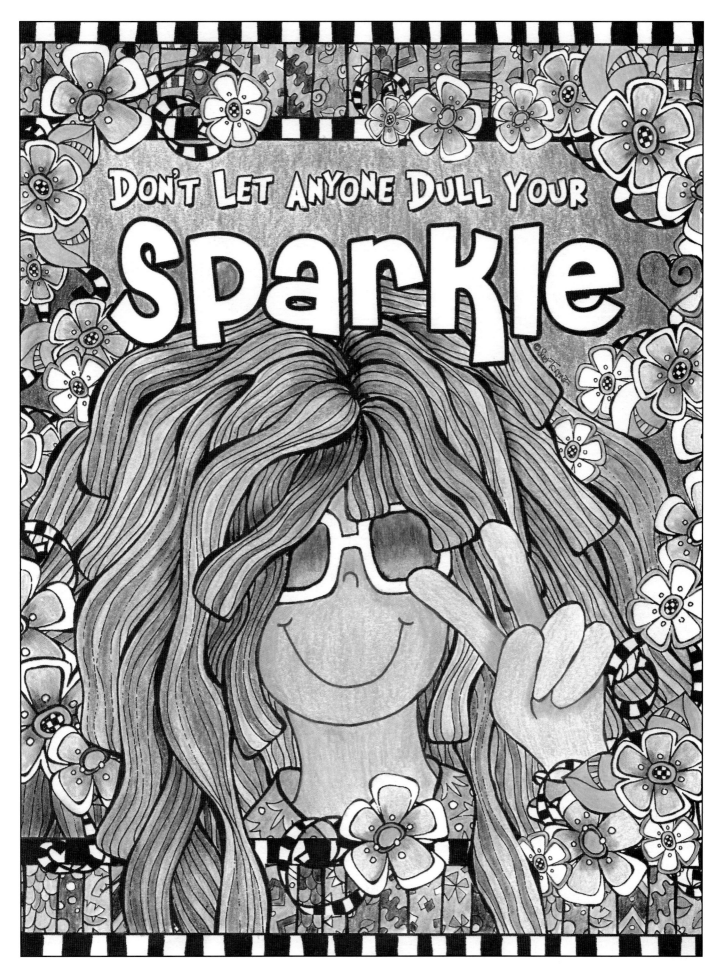

Don't Let Anyone Dull Your Sparkle (Light & Laughter), Color by Tina Sanders

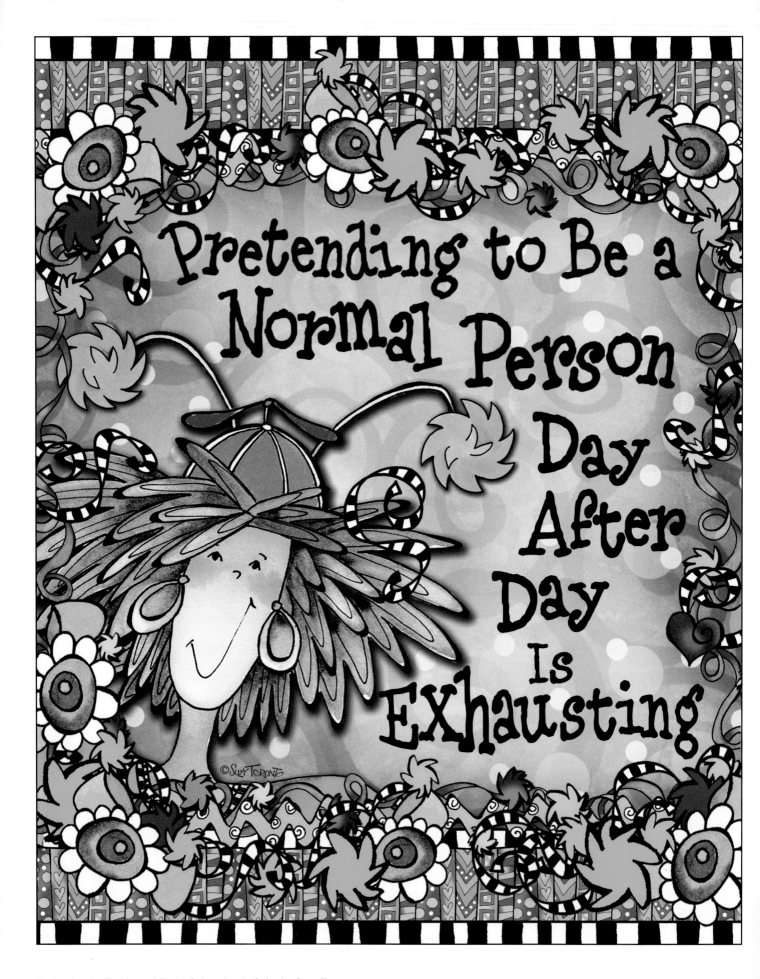

Pretending to Be a Normal Person Day After Day Is Exhausting

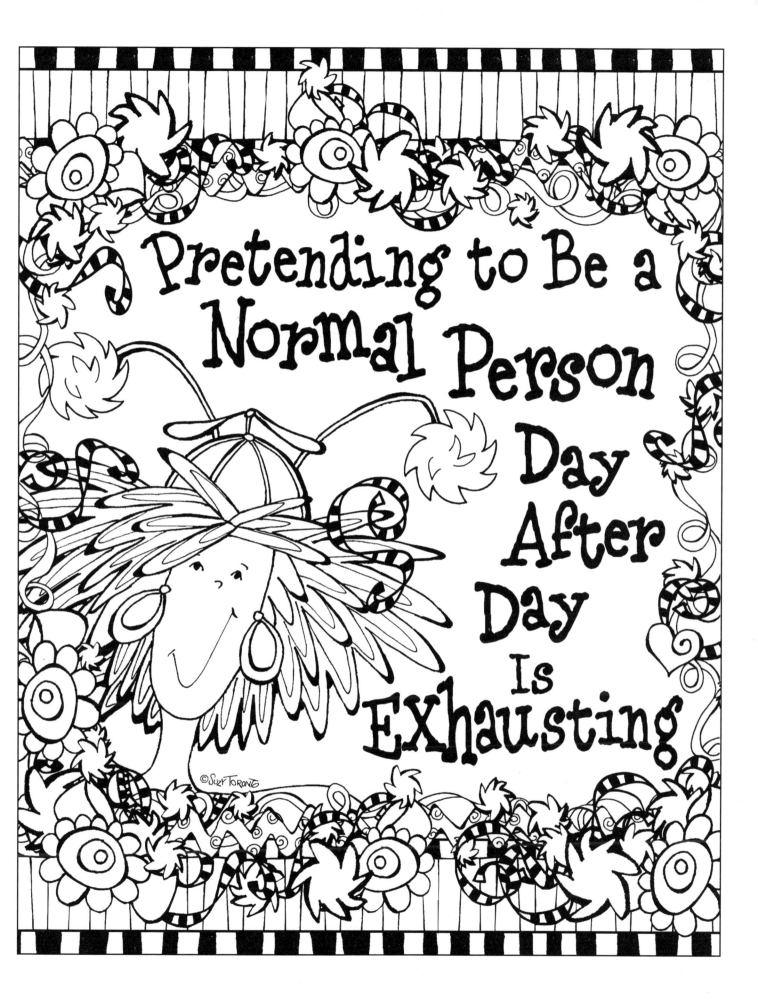

Let go of the status quo.
Decide just to be yourself.

Pretending to Be Normal (Light & Laughter)

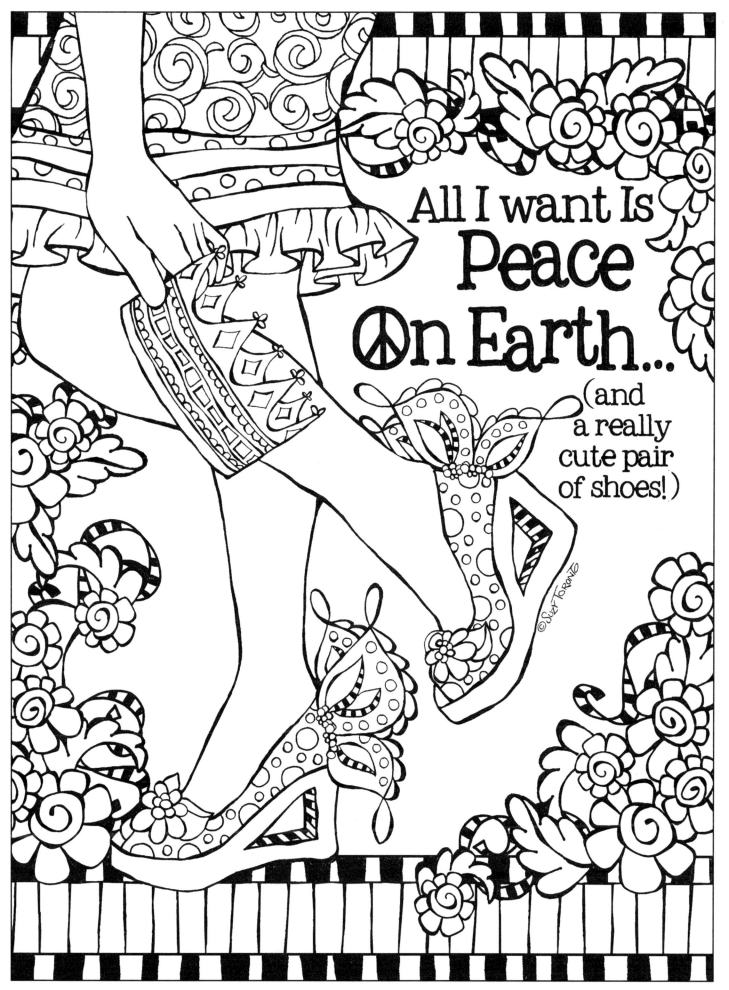

All I want Is **Peace On Earth...**
(and a really cute pair of shoes!)

Peace on Earth begins with
a bubble bath.

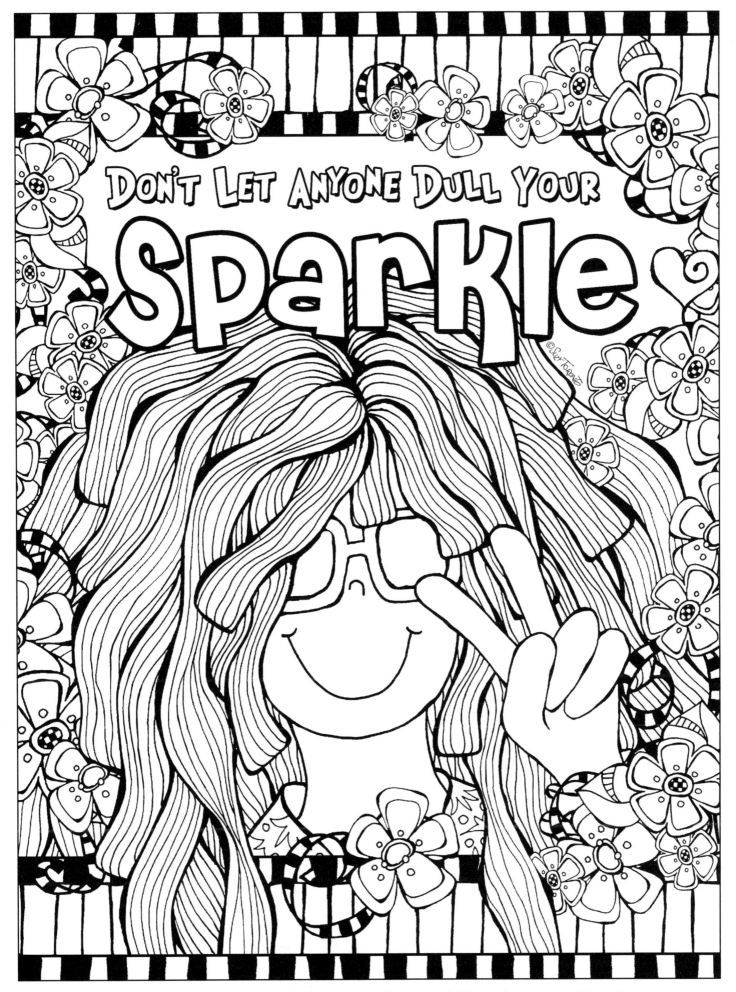

Always radiate sunshine. Life is too
short to be gloomy.

Don't Let Anyone Dull Your Sparkle (Light & Laughter)

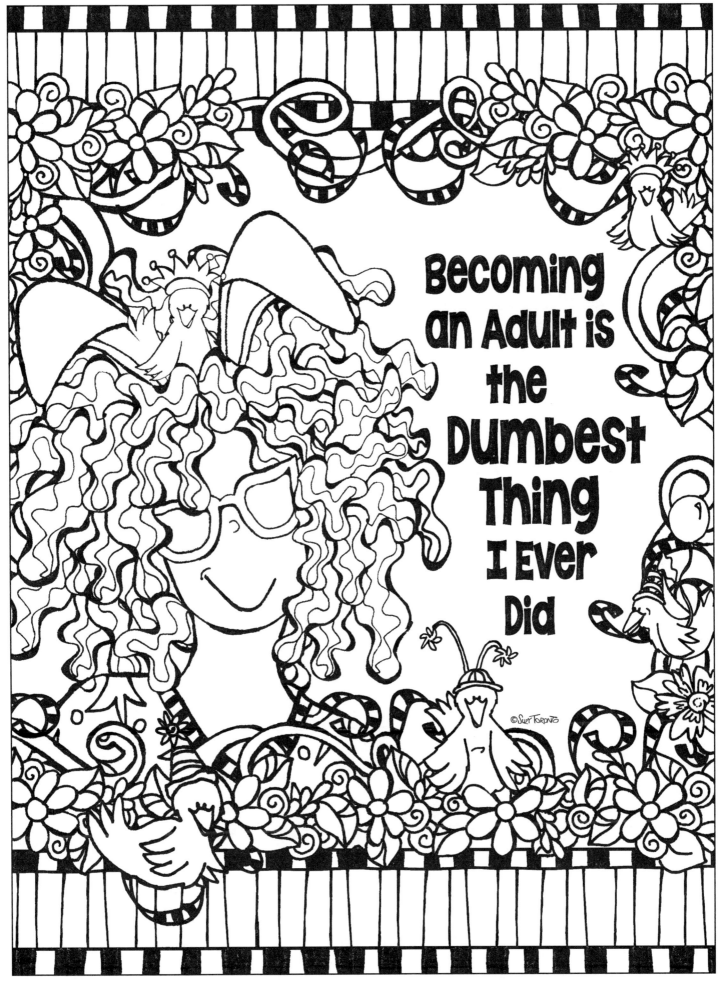

Becoming an Adult is the Dumbest Thing I Ever Did

I wonder when everyone is going
to catch on to the fact that I am only
pretending to be an adult.

_____
_____
_____
_____
_____
_____
_____
_____
_____

Becoming an Adult

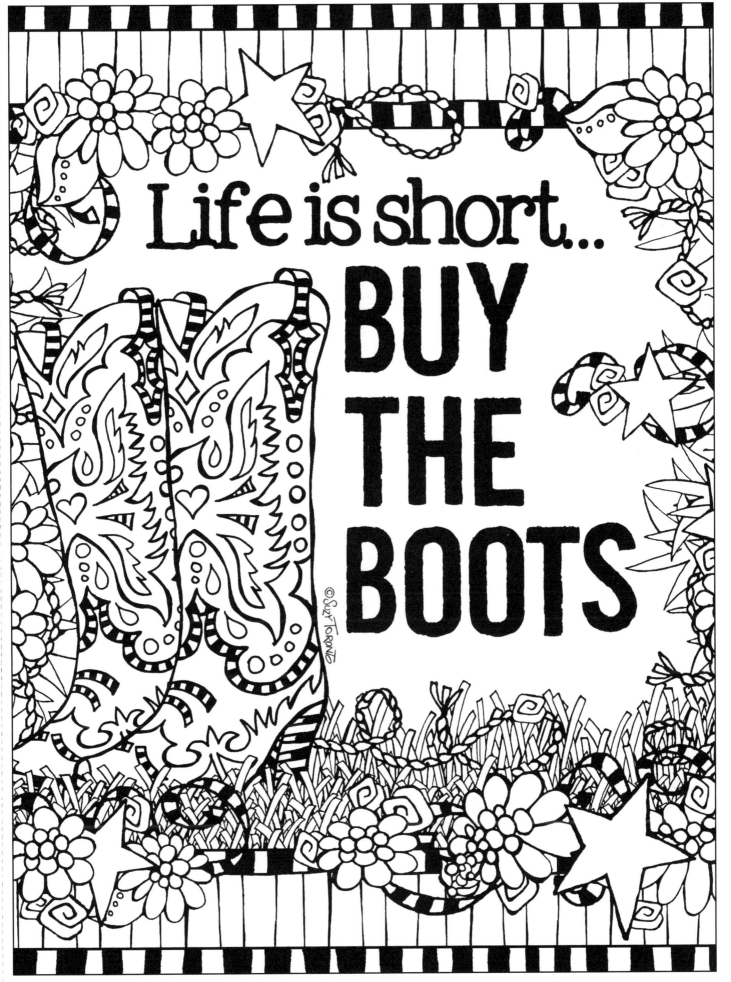

Life is short... BUY THE BOOTS

©Suzy Toronto

Embrace life and beam like you were
born with glitter in your veins.

_____
_____
_____
_____
_____
_____
_____
_____
_____
_____
_____

Buy the Boots

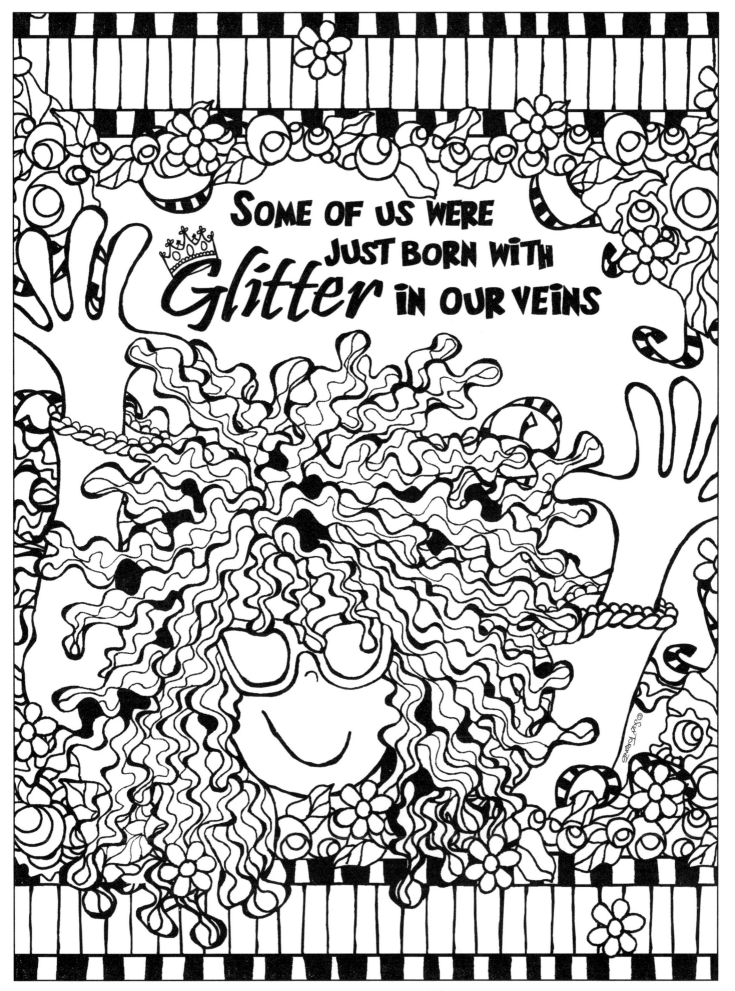

SOME OF US WERE JUST BORN WITH *Glitter* IN OUR VEINS

Put on some lipstick and
go rock the world.

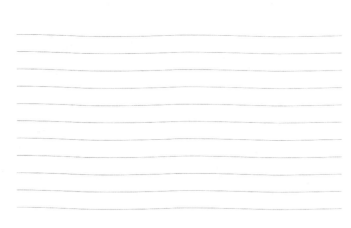

Born with Glitter

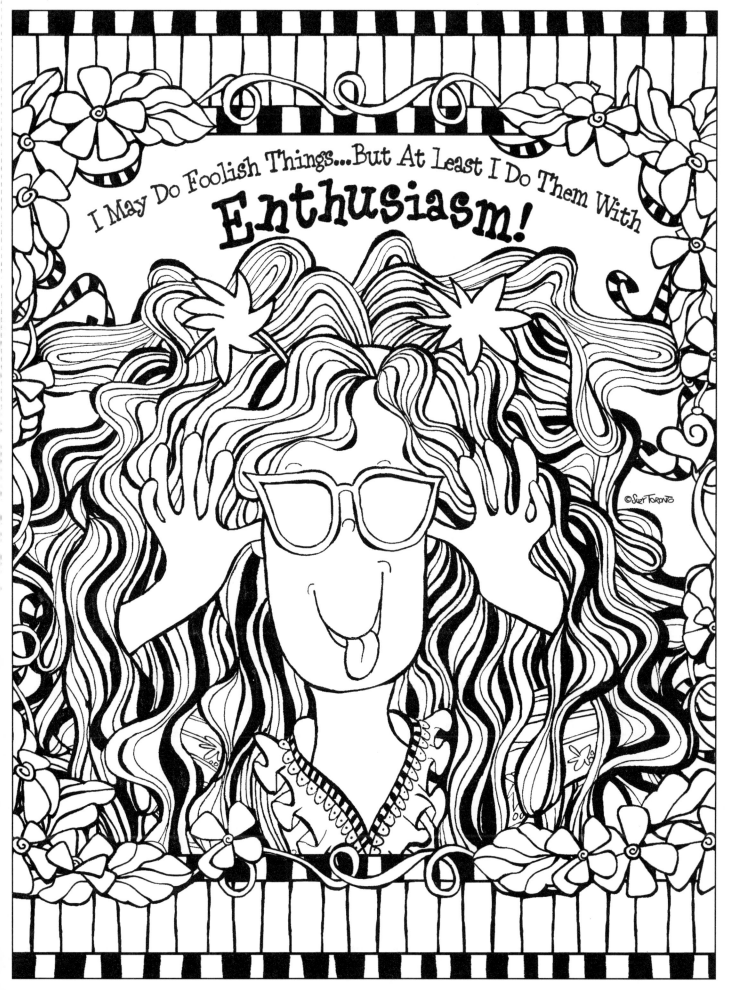

Don't be afraid to be a fruit loop in a world full of bran.

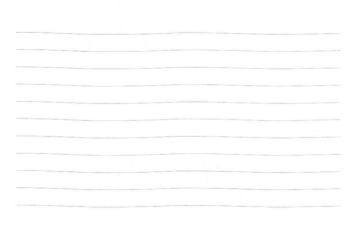

I Do Foolish Things with Great Enthusiasm
(Light & Laughter)

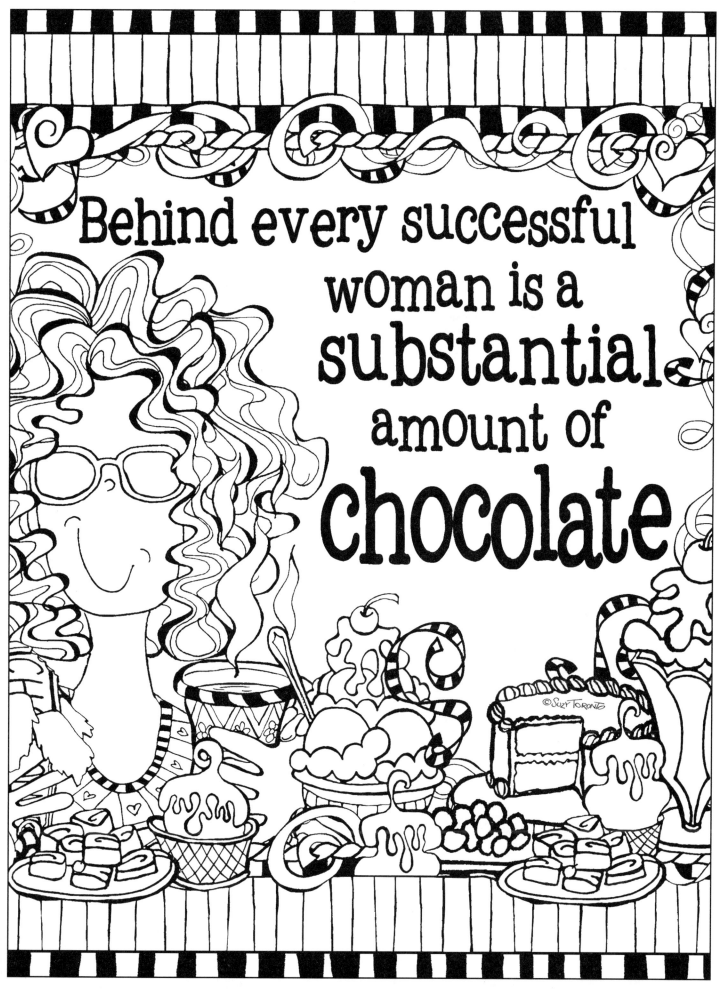

Behind every successful woman is a **substantial** amount of **chocolate**

Save the Earth. It's the only
planet with chocolate.

_____
_____
_____
_____
_____
_____
_____
_____
_____

Chocolate (Light & Laughter)

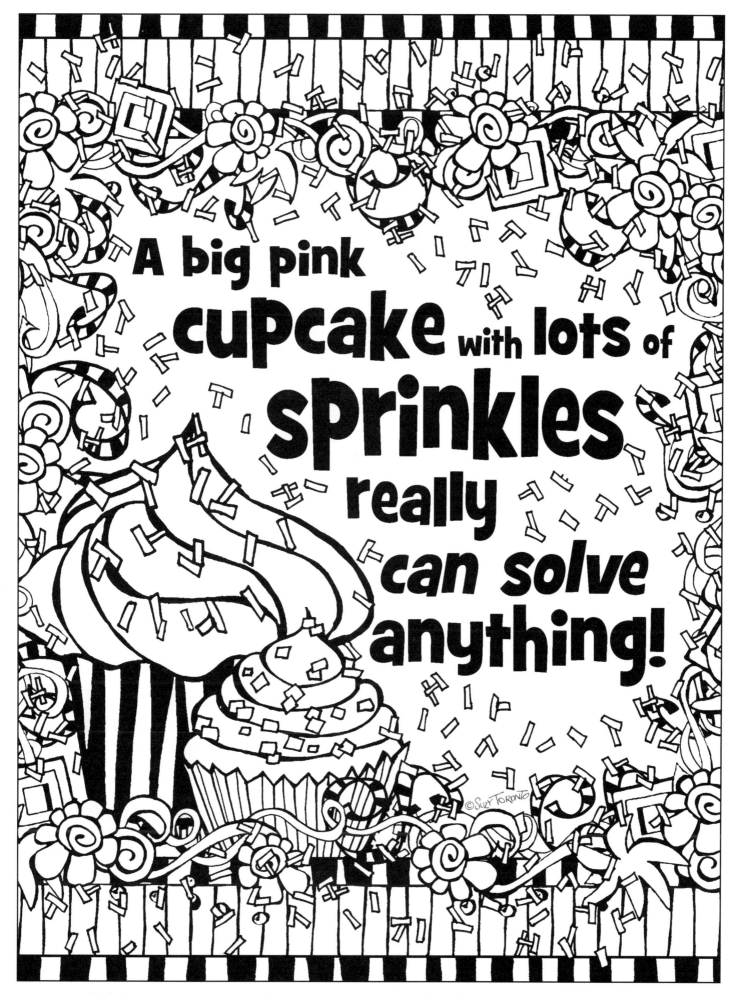

A big pink cupcake with lots of sprinkles really can solve anything!

Wish, hope, dream,
then eat a cupcake.

_____
_____
_____
_____
_____
_____
_____
_____
_____
_____

Big Pink Cupcake

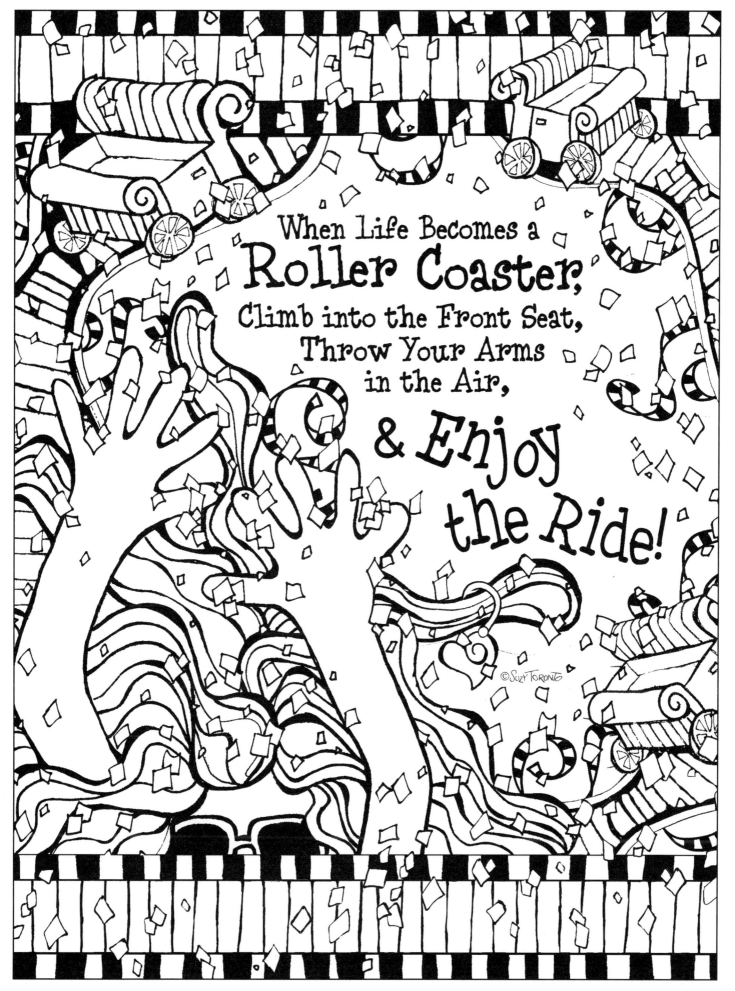

When Life Becomes a
Roller Coaster,
Climb into the Front Seat,
Throw Your Arms
in the Air,

& Enjoy
the Ride!

©Suzy Toronto

When everything around you seems to
be going up in flames, make s'mores.

Enjoy the Ride (Light & Laughter)

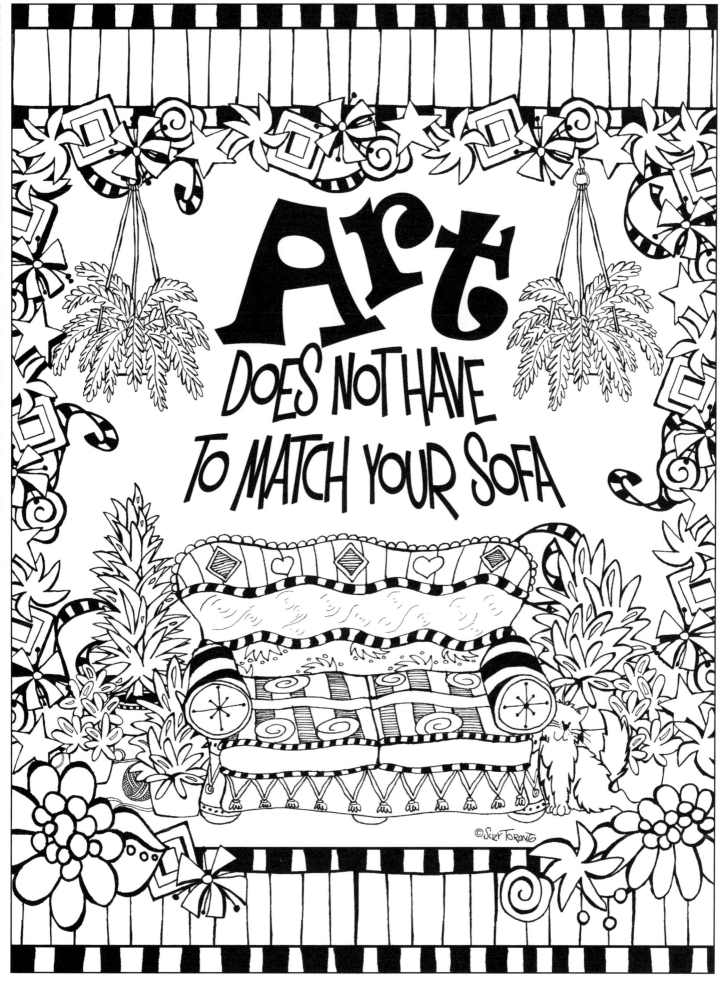

Art is not meant to decorate your
home, it's meant to decorate your soul.

_____
_____
_____
_____
_____
_____
_____
_____
_____
_____
_____
_____

Art

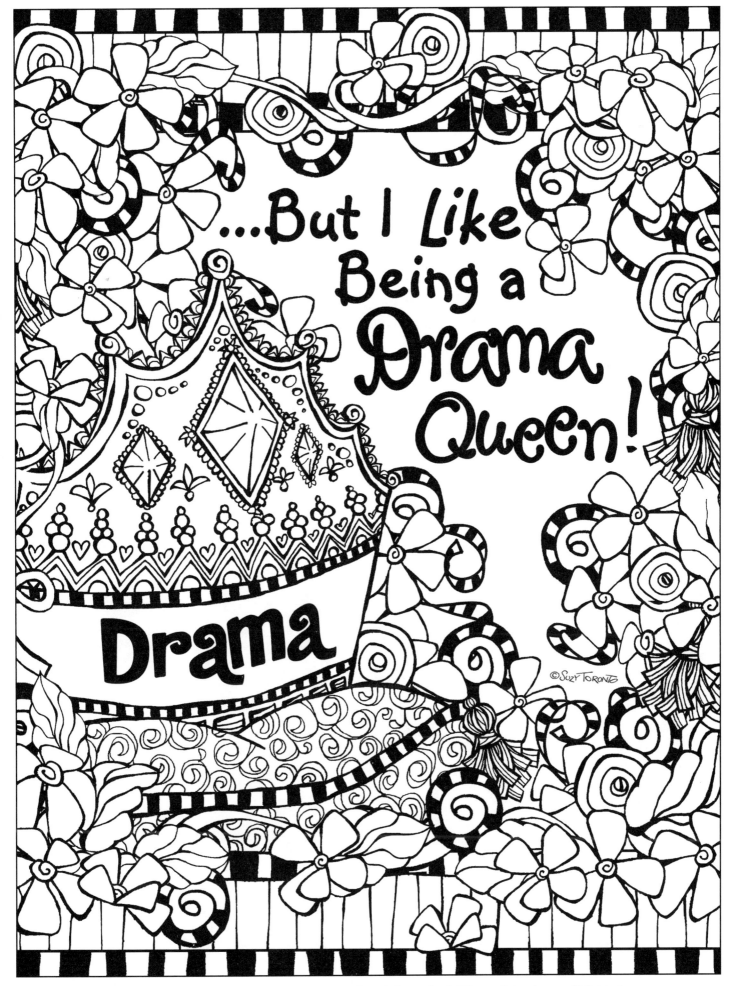

...But I Like Being a Drama Queen!

Drama

©Suzy Toronto

Oh yeah, no doubt about it.
I'm a legend in my own mind.

_____
_____
_____
_____
_____
_____
_____
_____
_____
_____

Drama Queen (Light & Laughter)

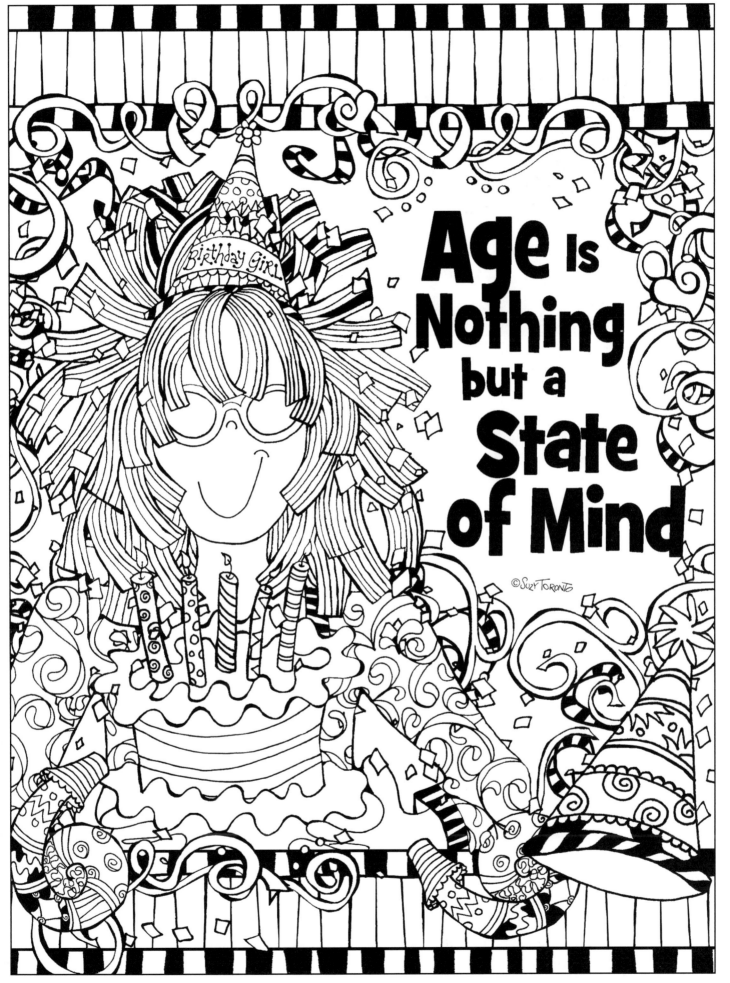

Age Is Nothing but a State of Mind

©Suzy Toronto

Inches and ages and sizes are just numbers, and numbers don't tell you anything about the amazing woman inside.

_____
_____
_____
_____
_____
_____
_____
_____
_____
_____

A State of Mind (Light & Laughter)

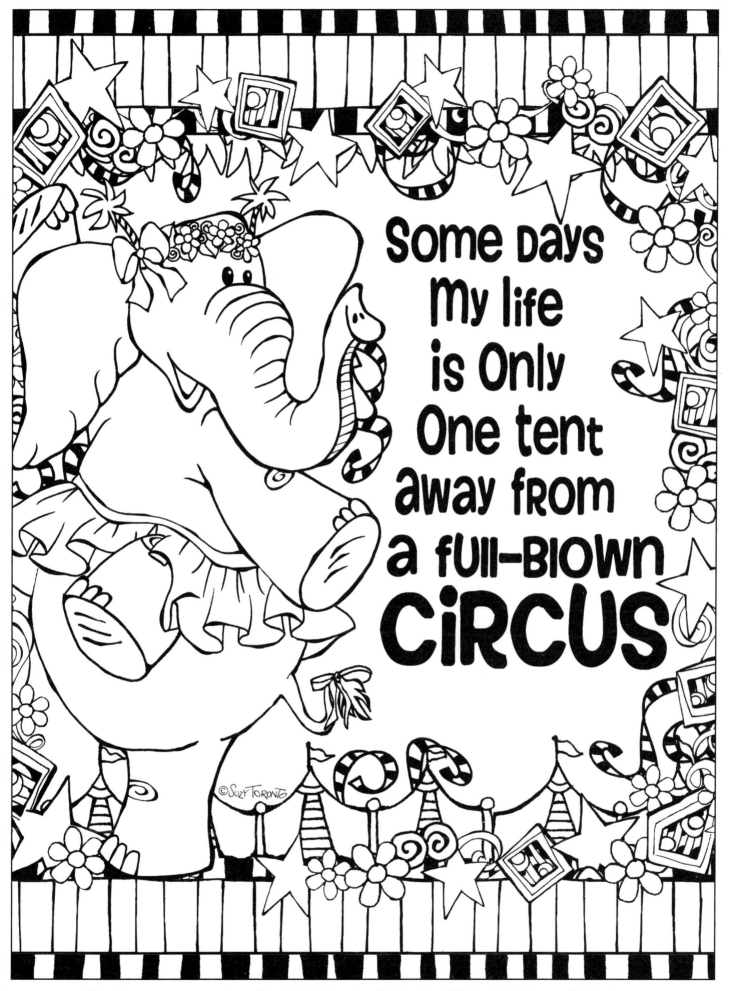

Some days My life is Only One tent away from a full-blown CIRCUS

©Suzy Toronto

You were given this life because
you are wacky enough to live
every minute of it.

_____
_____
_____
_____
_____
_____
_____
_____
_____

The Circus

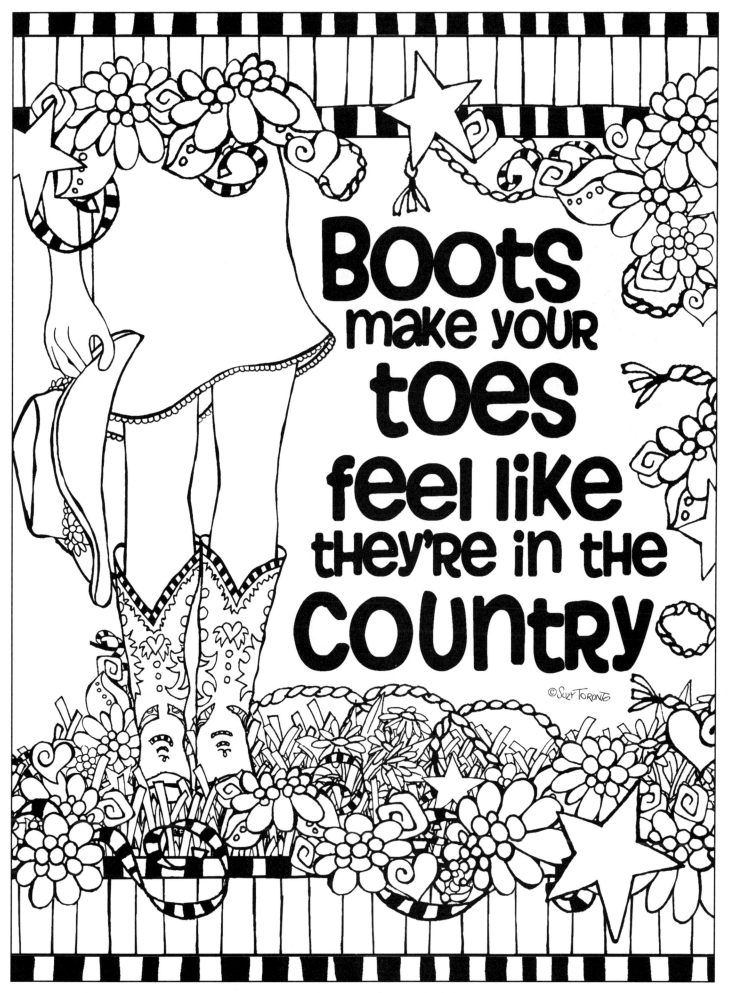

Boots make your toes feel like they're in the country

©Suzy Toronto

Life is a lot easier if you have a twinkle
in your eye and a smile on your face.

_____
_____
_____
_____
_____
_____
_____
_____

Country Boots

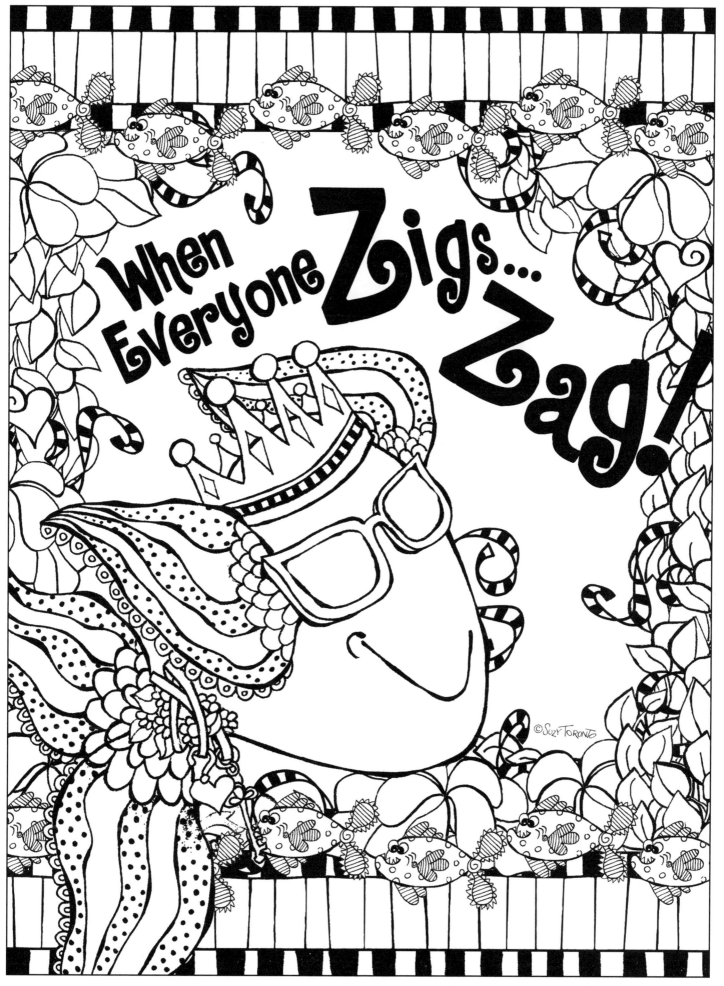

Absolutely over-the-top people
don't just happen, they evolve.

_____

_____

_____

_____

_____

_____

_____

_____

Zig Zag

Reading Is Like Dreaming with Your Eyes Wide Open

The Book of Life

Literature
Romance
Historical Fiction
Suspense
Adventure
Self Help
HUMOR

Don't talk about your dreams, live them.

_____
_____
_____
_____
_____
_____
_____
_____
_____
_____

Reading Is Like Dreaming (Light & Laughter)

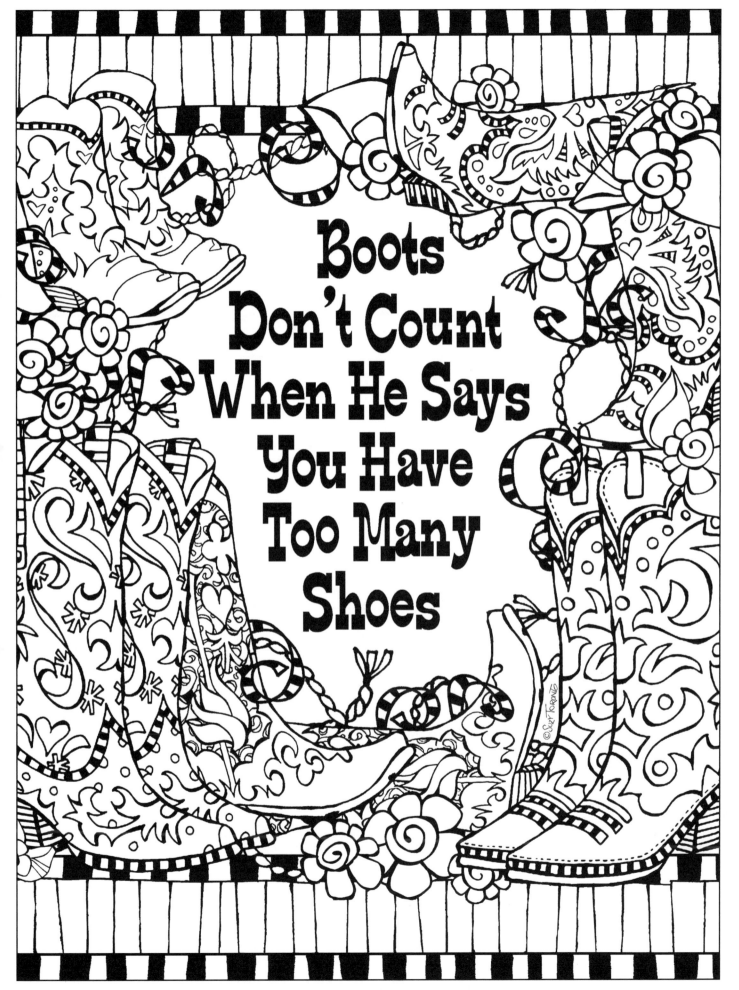

Boots
Don't Count
When He Says
You Have
Too Many
Shoes

Don't just give your next idea
a little hop. Plunge into it
with everything you've got.

_____
_____
_____
_____
_____
_____
_____

Too Many Shoes

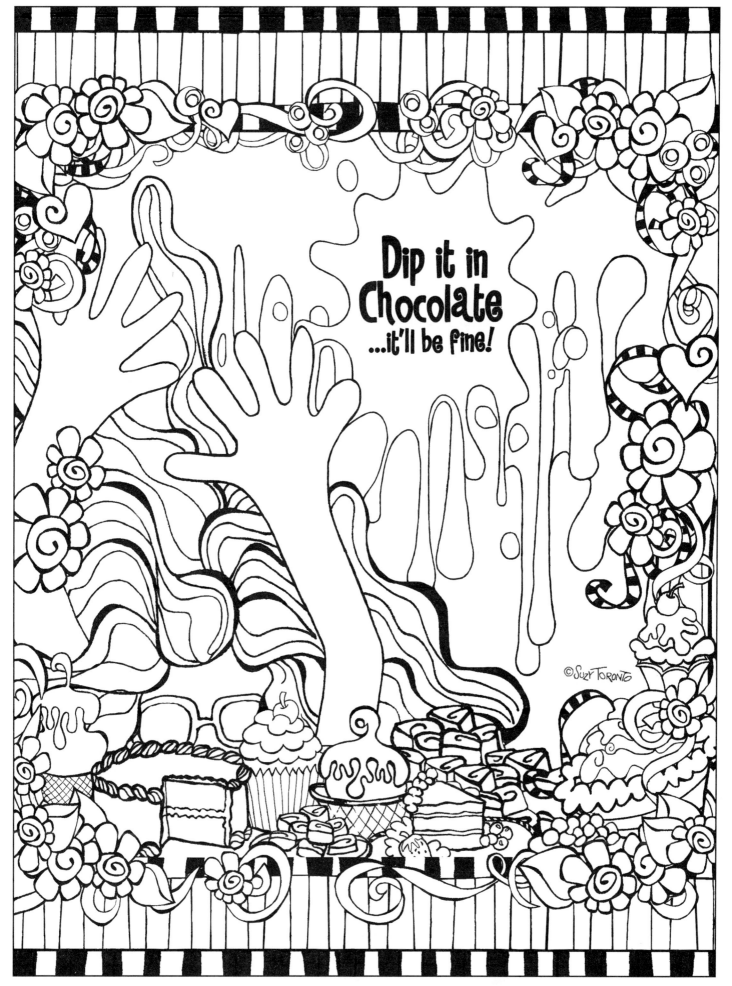

Dip it in
Chocolate
...it'll be fine!

©Suzy Toronto

The taste of rice cakes significantly improves when dipped in hot fudge.

Dip It in Chocolate

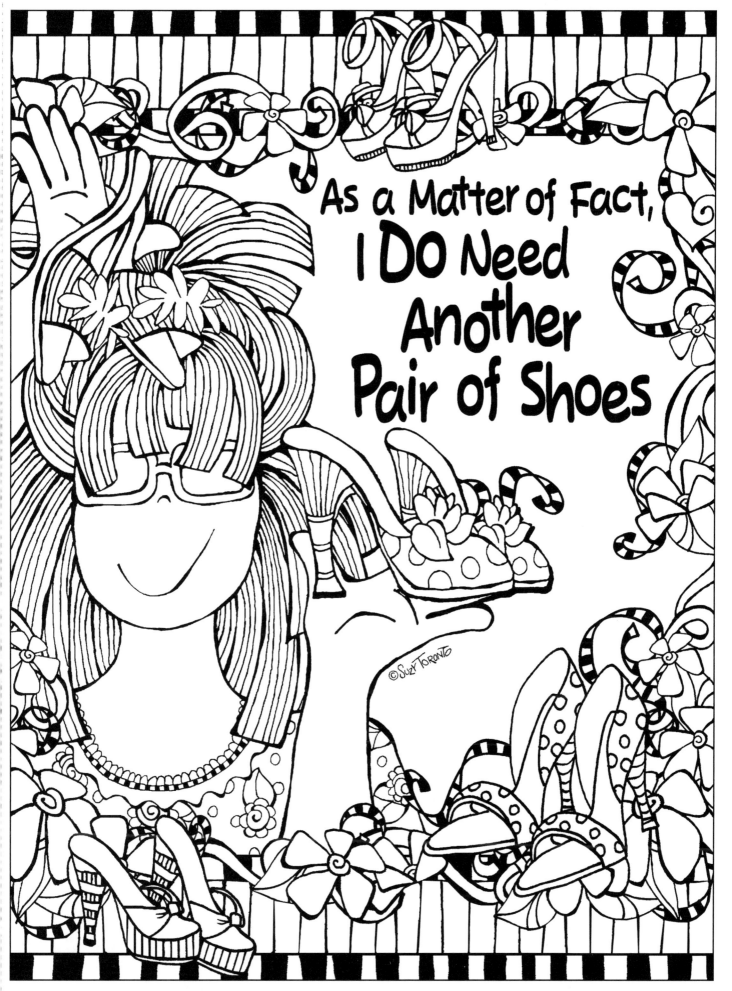

I MUST have cute shoes to survive!
It's a genetic predisposition carved
deep into my DNA.

_____
_____
_____
_____
_____
_____
_____
_____
_____
_____

Another Pair of Shoes (Light & Laughter)

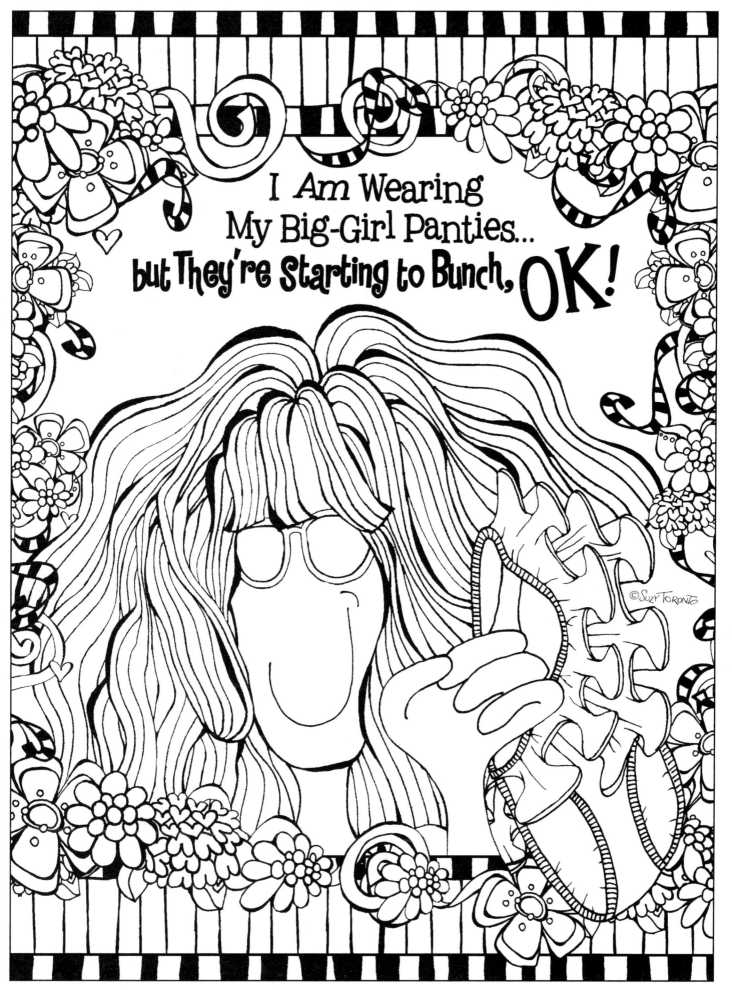

Have the faith and conviction
that you can do anything.

_____
_____
_____
_____
_____
_____
_____
_____
_____
_____

Big-Girl Panties (Light & Laughter)

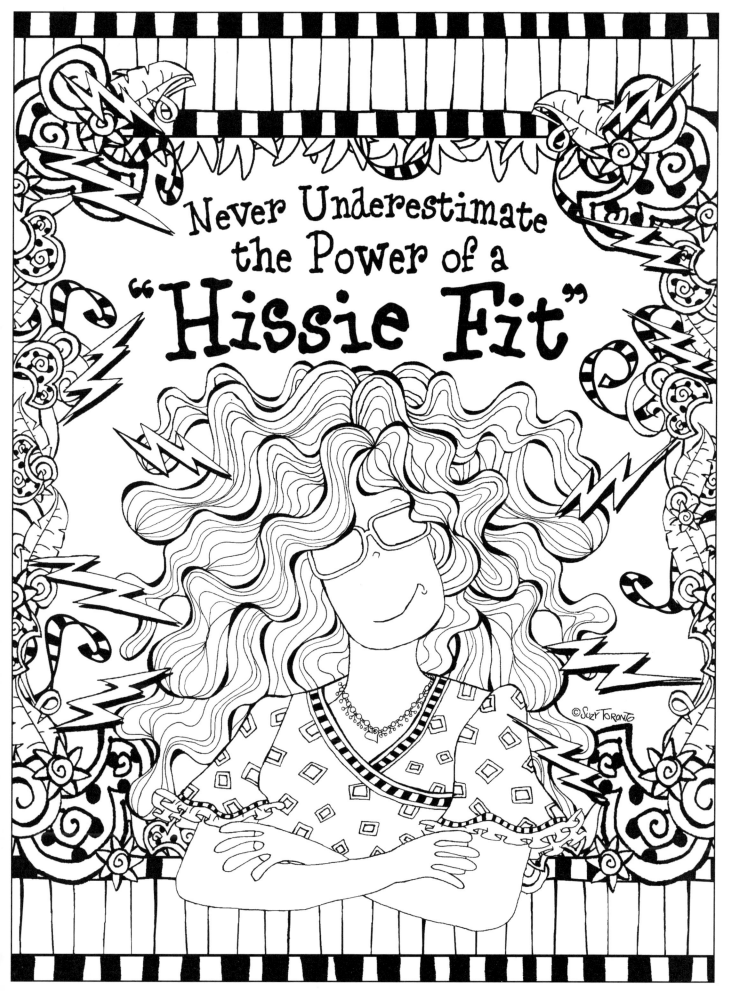

Some battles are worth the fight—
choose wisely.

Hissie Fit (Light & Laughter)

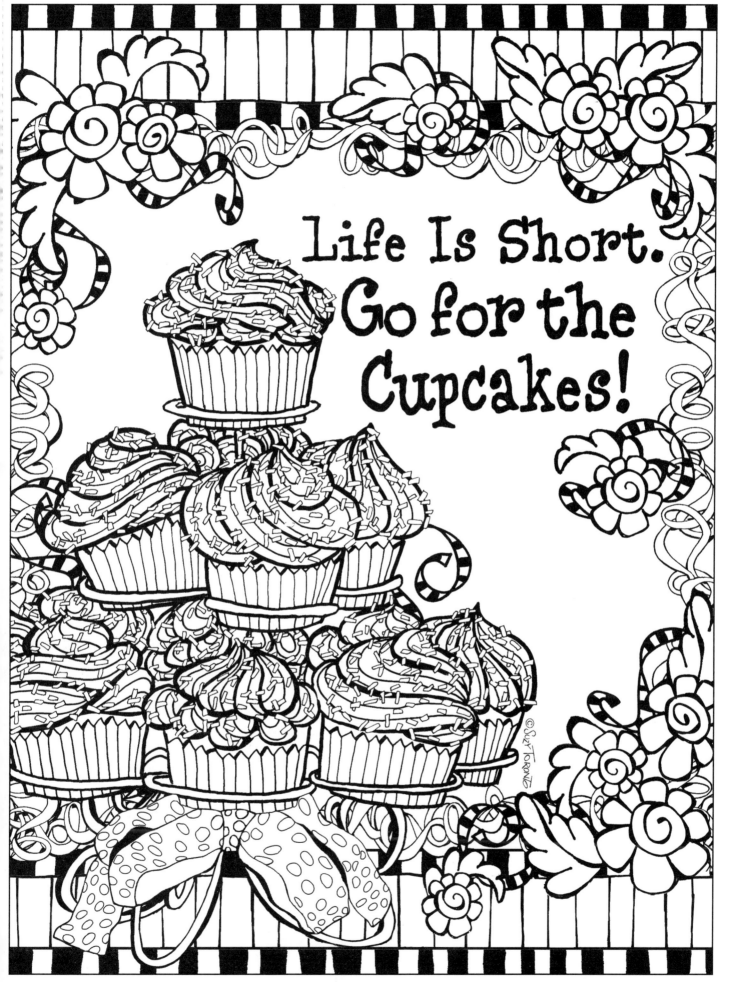

Life Is Short. Go for the Cupcakes!

Never underestimate the power of a
cupcake to make someone smile.

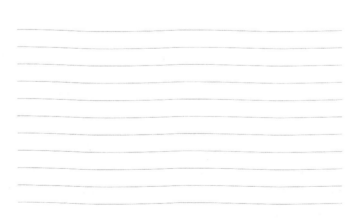

Go for the Cupcakes!

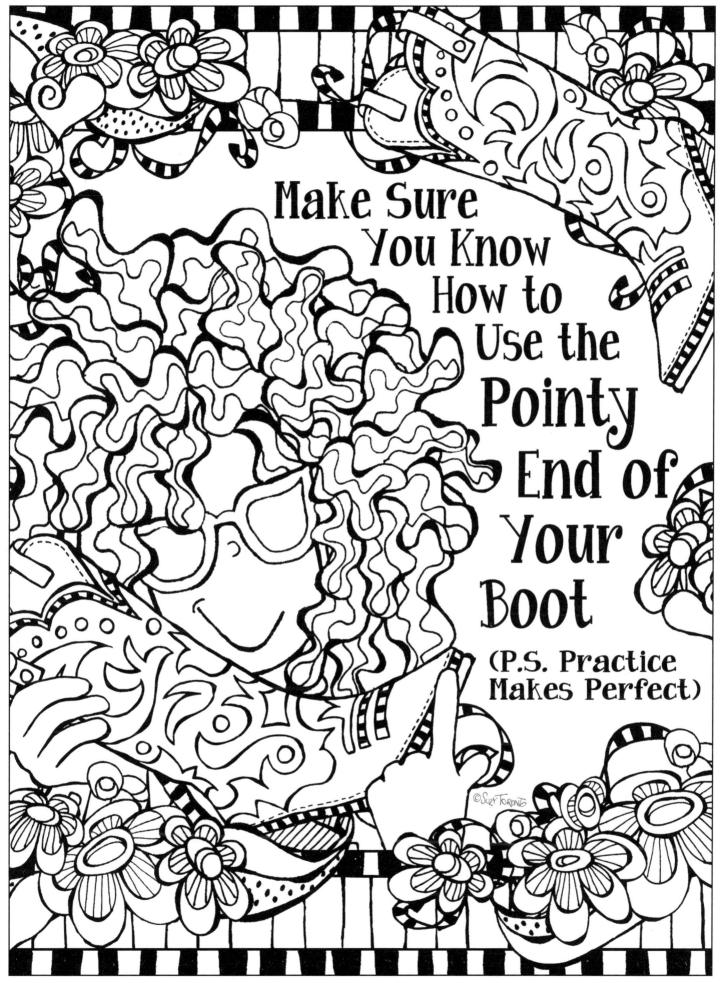

Make Sure You Know How to Use the Pointy End of Your Boot

(P.S. Practice Makes Perfect)

Don't be a willow in the wind. Stand tall.
Be strong. Carry yourself with
confidence, even if you have to
fake it 'til you make it.

_____
_____
_____
_____
_____
_____
_____
_____
_____
_____

The Pointy End

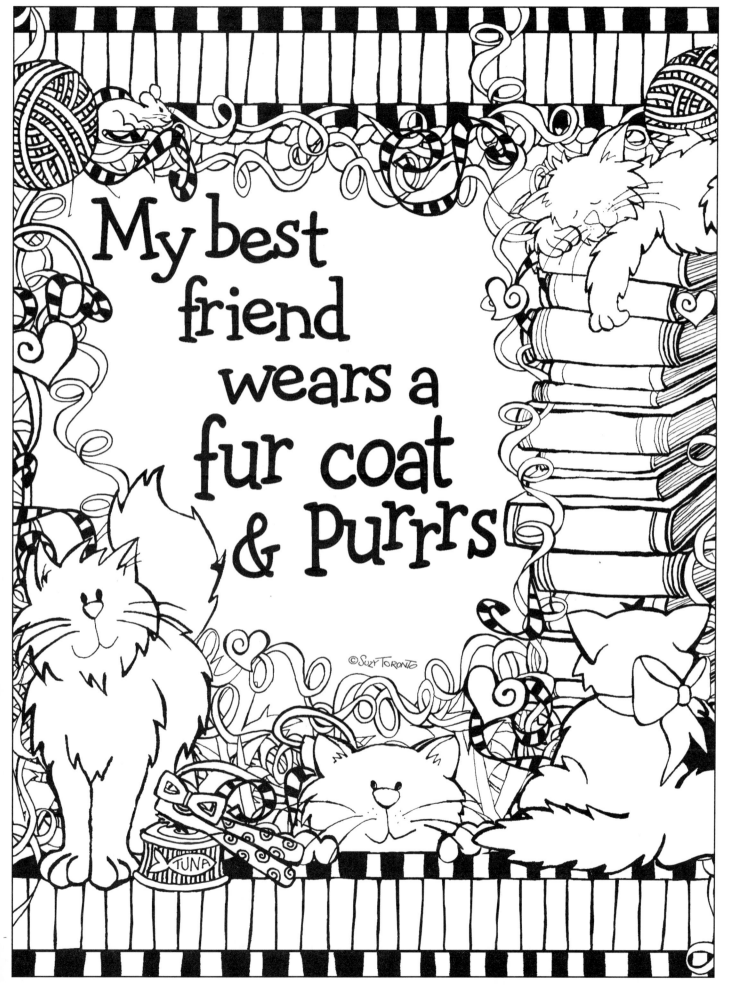

My best friend wears a fur coat & purrs

©Suzy Toronto

Some days I feel one meow short of
being the Crazy Cat Lady.

_____
_____
_____
_____
_____
_____
_____
_____

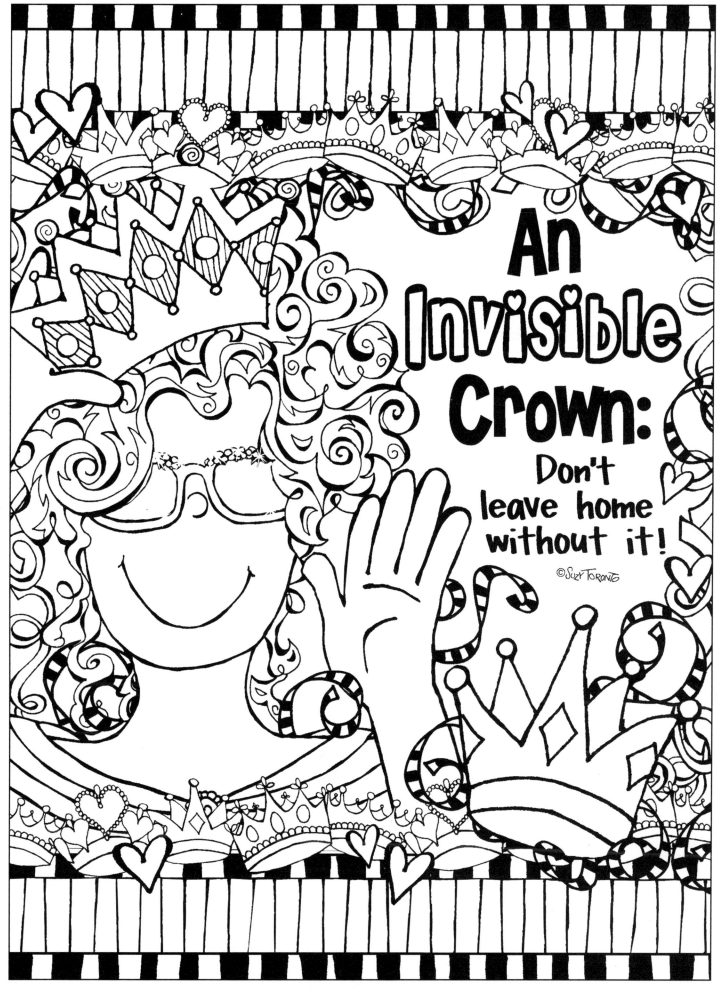

An Invisible Crown:
Don't leave home without it!

©Suzy Toronto

Put on your superhero shirt,
and be a wonder of a woman.

_____
_____
_____
_____
_____
_____
_____
_____
_____
_____

Invisible Crown

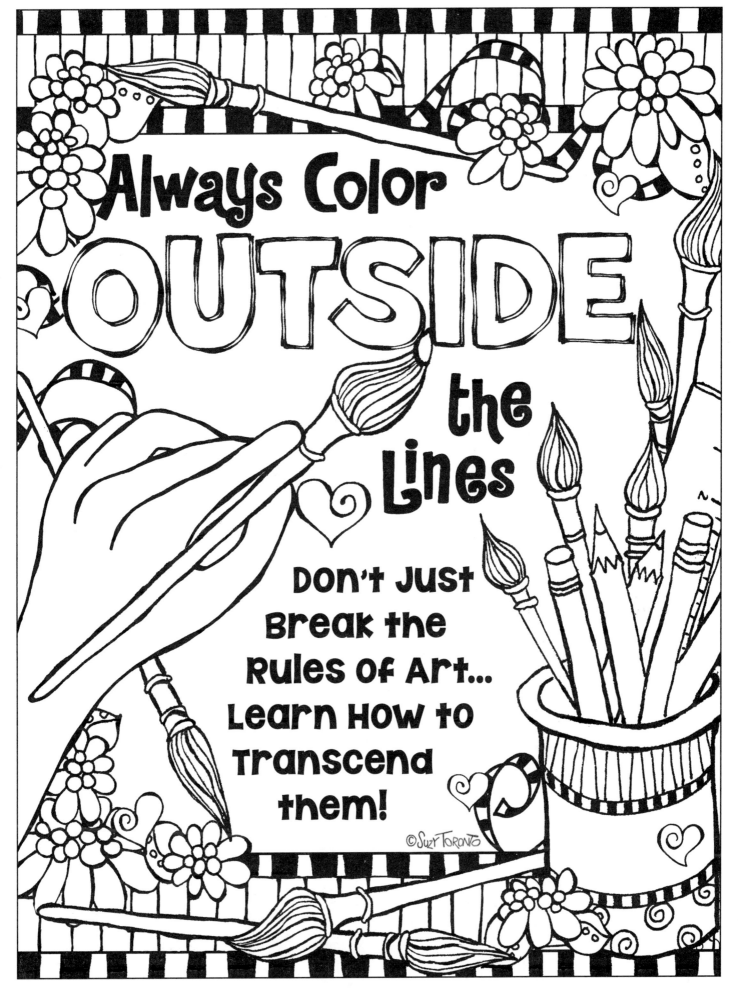

Always Color OUTSIDE the Lines

Don't just Break the Rules of Art... Learn How to Transcend them!

©Suzy Toronto

Life is about using the entire box of crayons and not worrying about keeping them all pointy.

_____
_____
_____
_____
_____
_____
_____
_____
_____
_____

Color Outside the Lines (Light & Laughter)

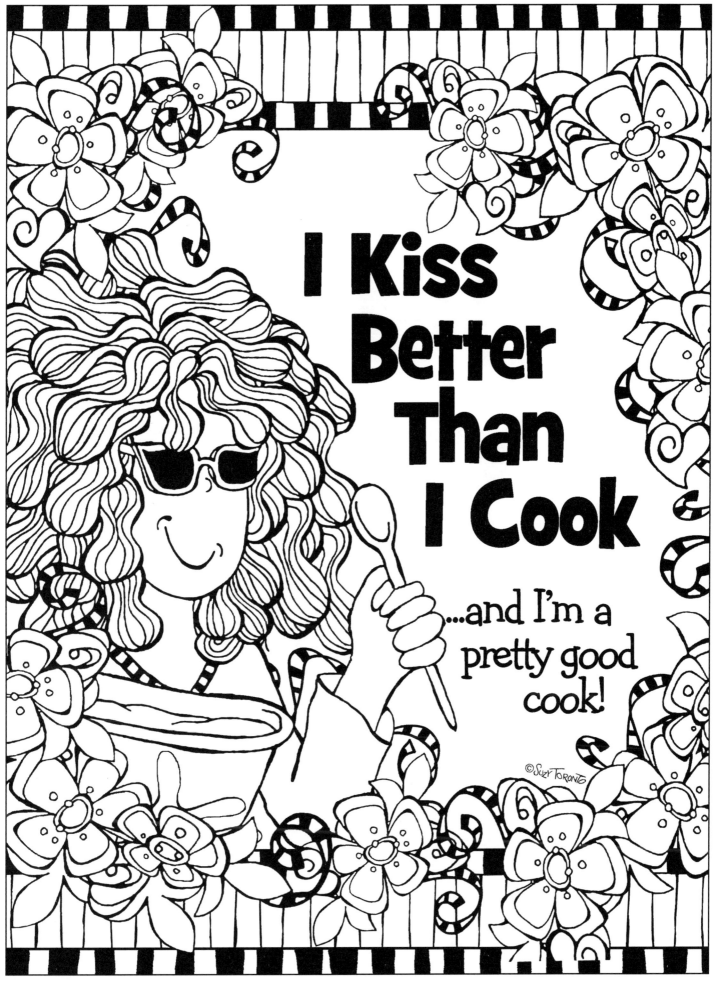

I Kiss Better Than I Cook

...and I'm a pretty good cook!

©Suzy Toronto

Kiss like you mean it, and always be
a hug waiting to happen.

_____
_____
_____
_____
_____
_____
_____
_____
_____

Kiss and Cook

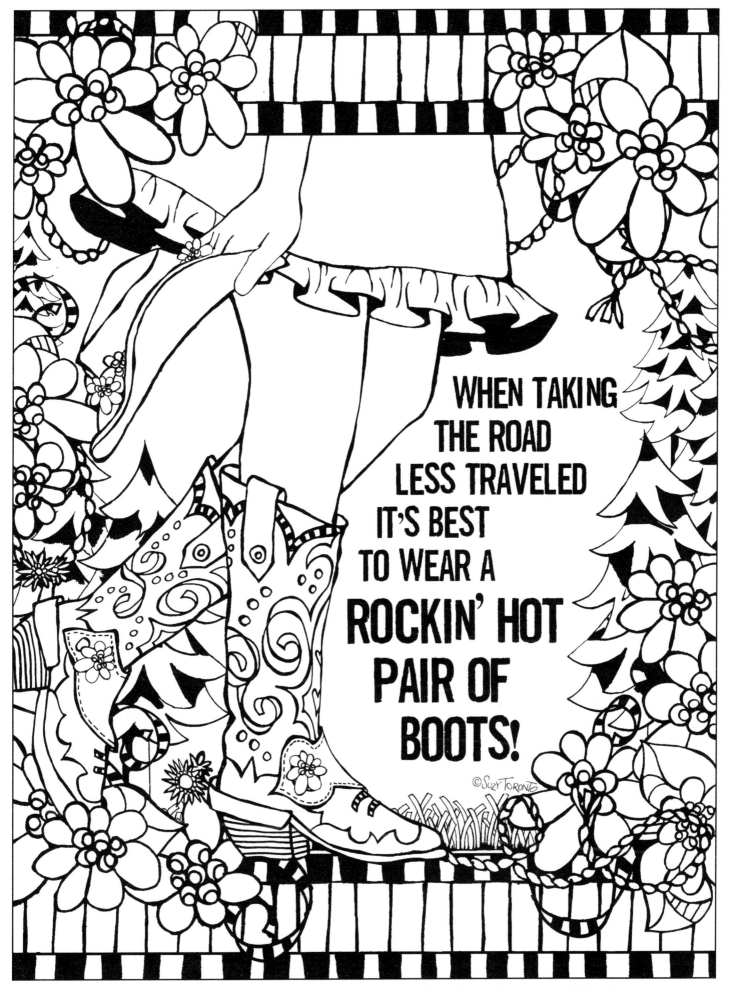

WHEN TAKING
THE ROAD
LESS TRAVELED
IT'S BEST
TO WEAR A
ROCKIN' HOT
PAIR OF
BOOTS!

©Suzy Toronto

Decide to fully live every day of
your life. The choice is yours.

_____
_____
_____
_____
_____
_____
_____
_____
_____
_____
_____

Road Less Traveled

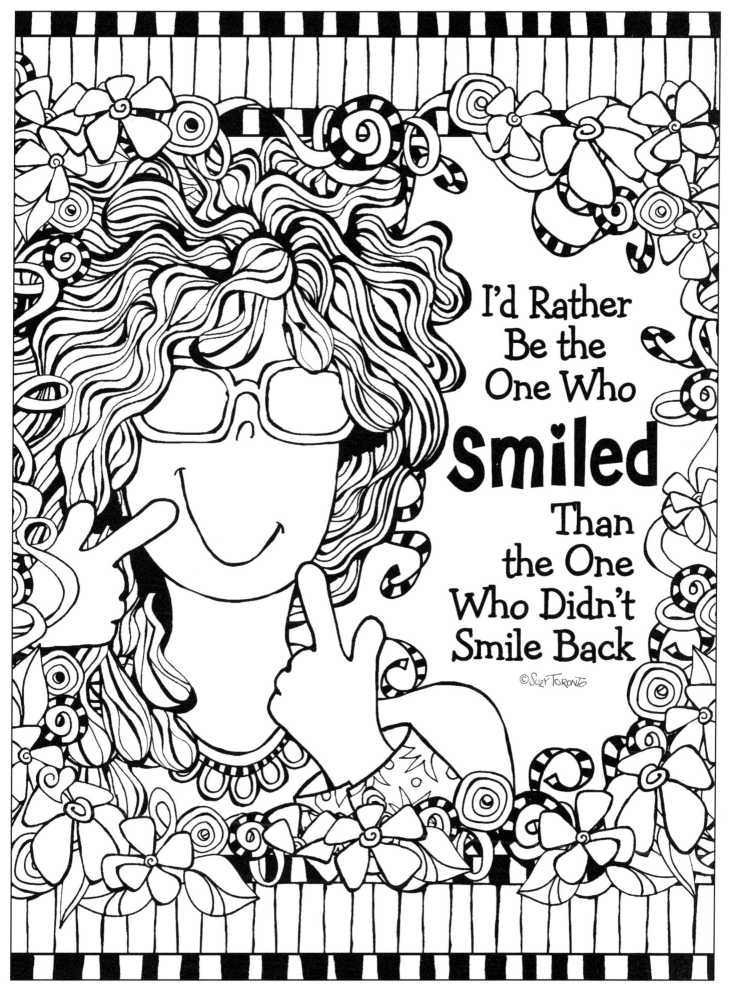

I'd Rather Be the One Who **Smiled** Than the One Who Didn't Smile Back

©Suzy Toronto

Be responsible for the mojo
you bring into the room.

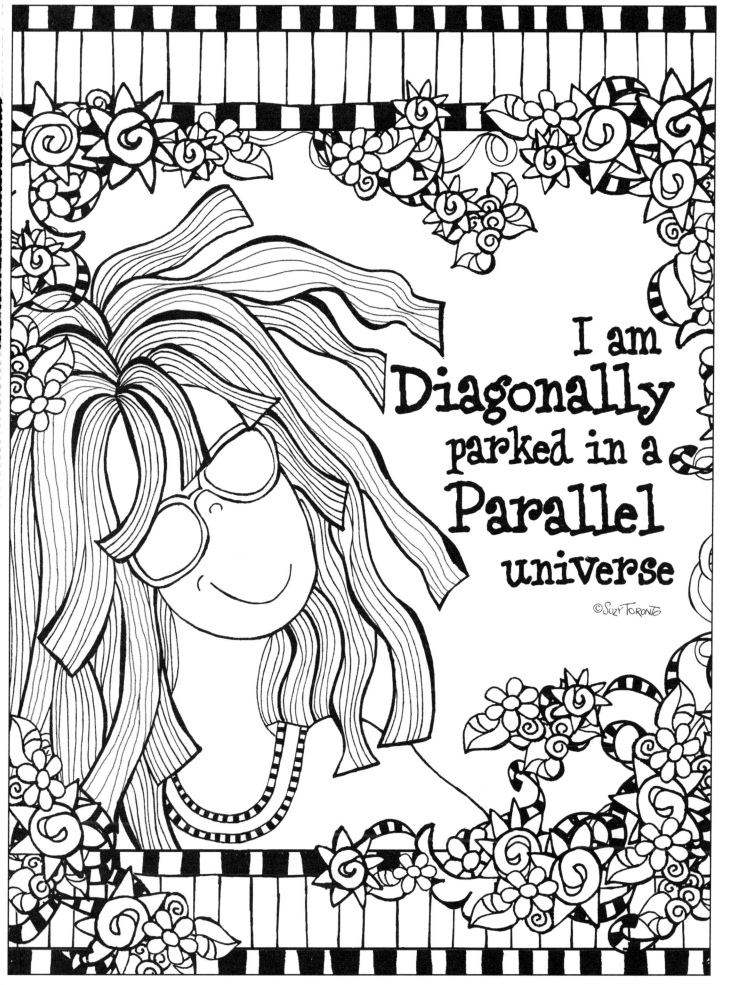

I am Diagonally parked in a Parallel universe

©Suzy Toronto

I like it when things are upside down
and inside out. It makes life interesting.

Diagonally Parked